This Land Is Our Land

Immigrants and Power in Miami

Alex Stepick
Guillermo Grenier
Max Castro
Marvin Dunn

UNIVERSITY OF CALIFORNIA PRESS

Berkeley   Los Angeles   London

University of California Press
Berkeley and Los Angeles, California

University of California Press, Ltd.
London, England

© 2003 by the Regents of the University of California

Library of Congress Cataloging-in-Publication Data

   This land is our land : immigrants and power in Miami /
Alex Stepick . . . [et al.].

     p.   cm.
   Includes bibliographical references and index.
   ISBN 0–520–23397–2 (alk. paper)—ISBN 0–520–23398–0
(pbk. : alk. paper)
     1. Miami (Fla.)—Ethnic relations.   2. Miami (Fla.)—
Politics and government.   3. Miami (Fla.)—Economic
conditions.   4. Immigrants—Florida—Miami—Social
conditions.   5. Minorities—Florida—Miami—Social
conditions.   6. Cuban Americans—Florida—Miami—
Social conditions.   7. Elite (Social sciences)—Florida—
Miami.   8. Power (Social sciences)—Florida—Miami.
9. Ethnic conflict—Florida—Miami.   I. Stepick, Alex.

F319.M6T48   2003
305.8′009759′381—dc21

                          2002011201

Manufactured in the United States of America

12 11 10 09 08 07 06 05 04

10 9 8 7 6 5 4 3 2

The paper used in this publication is both acid-free and
totally chlorine-free (TCF). It meets the minimum
requirements of ANSI/NISO Z39.48–1992 (R 1997)
(Permanence of Paper). ⊗

CONTENTS

ACKNOWLEDGMENTS

We would like to thank all of those who gave us their time, experiences, and opinions. The Ford Foundation, and particularly William Díaz and Mary McClymont, provided the majority of the funding for the fieldwork. The Dade Foundation also provided financial support critical to the fieldwork. Subsequent research after the original Ford Foundation project was supported by grants from the National Science Foundation (SPB-9511515), the Andrew Mellon Foundation, the Carnegie Corporation, and the Spencer Foundation.

Numerous research assistants contributed mightily to gathering the data: Hilda Gutierrez Baldoquin, Sue Chaffee, Eddie Compas, Yetta Decklebaum, Charmane de Gannes, Debbie Draznin, Emmanuel Eugene, Hafidh M. Hafidh, Aline LaBorwit, Steve Morris, Peggy Nolan, and Christine Wines.

The project could not have been completed without the assistance and contributions of the Center for Labor Research and Studies at Florida International University. Greater Miami United donated services and materials that further advanced our work. In the community, especially helpful people included Pepe Collado, International Representative of the Carpenters Union; the staff and teachers at Miami Edison

High school, particularly the principal, Craig Sturgeon, and the teachers in the English and English as a Second Language departments; the staff of the Greater Miami Chamber of Commerce (GMCC); and Florida International University's president, Mitch Maidique, who helped us gain access to GMCC and community leaders. We agreed to maintain the anonymity of many who cooperated with us and must thank the remainder indirectly. The management of the apparel factory where we conducted research was extraordinarily open, kind, and helpful. The students at Miami Edison also assisted us far beyond the minimum. Carol Stepick provided editorial advice, and we wish we could have given her more time to further improve our writing. Whatever errors remain are entirely the responsibility of the four co-investigators.

ONE

Becoming American
It's Not a One-Way Street

On Thanksgiving Day 1999, a six-year-old boy, Elián González, was found floating on an inner tube three miles off the Florida coast. He was reportedly surrounded by dolphins and, more surprisingly, in spite of being in the water for three days, he was not sunburned at all. The U. S. Coast Guard spotted the boy, along with the two other survivors of a vessel that had been carrying fourteen passengers from Cuba. The other eleven, including the boy's mother, had apparently drowned. The Coast Guard immediately transferred Elián to Joe DiMaggio Children's Hospital. The two other survivors were rescued after they swam to Key Biscayne, a few miles from downtown Miami.

Two days after the boy was found, Elián's father in Cuba declared that he wanted his son back. Under normal circumstances, the sole surviving parent's wishes are the last word on such matters. However, there is nothing normal about dealing with Cuba or Cuban Americans. Miami Cubans passionately argued that Elián's mother had died to give the boy freedom from Castro's dictatorship and that he should be permitted to stay in Miami with his great uncle, Lázaro González. After a considerable delay and interviews in Cuba with the boy's father, on January 6, 2000, Janet Reno announced, "This little boy, who has been through so much, belongs with his father." It was not only the little boy who went through so much during those six months; the community where the events unfolded would never be the same either. The drama preceding and following this decision cemented, in the eyes of the nation and the world, Miami's reputation as a city deeply divided along ethnic lines, where ethnicity and immigration combine to create an unstable fulcrum of power and prejudice, and where new arrivals to this country, rather than being disenfranchised, are empowered enough to be regularly accused of prejudice against long-established residents. In this type of community, sometimes heralded as a preview to twenty-first-century United States, Elián's saga served as a magnifying glass, highlighting and at the same time kindling the tensions that have been building up over the past forty years of mass immigration into Miami.

The story of Elián González is worth recounting here, at the beginning of our volume, because it brought even the most peripheral citizens of the region face-to-face with profound issues of identity, power, and prejudice. For nearly everyone, African Americans, non-Hispanic whites, and many other immigrants, the overwhelming question raised by the months of taking sides over whether Elián should stay or go was, "What does it mean to be an American?" For Cuban Americans, even those who never held tightly to the typical anti-Castro dogma, the question became, "What does it mean to be a Cuban *in* America?"

After Reno announced the Justice Department's decision, Miami's Cuban community declared that it would unleash massive protests. "Let's take action immediately with the objective of paralyzing Miami and paralyzing the airport," urged Alberto Hernandez, a director of the Cuban American National Foundation, speaking to other leaders of the Cuban exile community at a meeting following the announcement. On January 6, hundreds of Miami's Cubans blocked intersections throughout the urban center and cut off access to the Port of Miami and the airport. The "political correctness" of Miami's Cuban community in demanding that Elián stay in the United States was transmitted throughout the world by Miami-Dade County mayor Alex Penelas, who proclaimed at a press conference that county law enforcement officers would not cooperate with the federal authorities in reuniting Elián with his father. If violence broke out, he warned the Clinton administration, "We hold you responsible." The county mayor's comments particularly alienated Miami's non-Cuban communities. At a Town Hall Meeting organized by ABC-TV's "Nightline" on the campus of Florida International University, a non-Cuban speaker from the audience chastised Mayor Penelas for his comments by reminding him that "he was elected to represent all of the citizens of Dade County."

Ultimately, the issue was resolved by force. Before the sun rose on Saturday, April 22, the day before Easter, agents of the Immigration and Naturalization Service (INS) stormed the house of Lázaro González to retrieve Elián. The small number of observers on the scene fortunately gave only token resistance to the well-armed strike force. Pictures of the raid circumnavigated the globe via internet, television, and newspapers. A few hours later, Elián was reunited with his father.

The Miami Cuban community vilified the U. S. government. A Miami Cuban professional in his late twenties exclaimed, "It's a betrayal. They betrayed us. We've been the most loyal supporters of the U. S. How could they do this?" A sobbing Bertha Garcia, a Cuban American who had lived in Miami for thirty-eight years, proclaimed, "I thought it was the most unbelievable thing that I've seen in my life in the United States done to a poor family with a poor house." Cuban American celebrities Gloria Estefan and Andy García expressed their support for Elián remaining in the United States. Even moderate, broad-based organizations like the Cuban-American National Council, criticized the government's strong-arm tactics in a public statement: "We know no precedent for such an extraordinary operation, and cannot understand why the Justice Department deployed a commando tactical force, armed with semiautomatic weapons, face masks, and tear gas, that broke into the home of an innocent American family, the same family that the Justice Department itself had previously entrusted with Elián's care." Seventy Cuban-American leaders of twenty-one exile organizations called for a citywide strike on the following Tuesday to "send a message of pain to the federal government and the nation about Elián's seizure." They sought to turn Miami into a "dead city."

Throughout the Latino sections of Miami, they had a dramatic effect. In the heart of Little Havana, along Calle Ocho, nearly all businesses were closed as they were in Hialeah, the most thoroughly Latino municipality. Crowds gathered on the sidewalks, and long convoys of vehicles slowed traffic, especially at key intersections. Vitriolic anti-government placards condemned the raid, calling Clinton a communist and Reno a lesbian. Cuban flags were everywhere; many also displayed the U. S. flag but flew it upside down.

"We are staying away from work as a way to express our outrage, not only over Elián but also against what we see as a major change in U. S. policy—one that indicates an improvement in relations with Fidel Castro," declared Carlos Rodriguez Nuñez, a retired paint-store owner who was one of the few pedestrians on Calle Ocho (officially Eighth Street), the main street of Little Havana. A Cuban American pediatrician closed his practice for the day. One of his sick patients visited a non-Cuban pediatrician for treatment. The non-Cuban pediatrician called the Cuban American pediatrician for information on the case. The Cuban pediatrician took advantage of the call to assail for nearly an hour the non-Cuban pediatrician for working that day, passionately declaiming that no one did or could understand the hurt and pain of exiled Cubans.

About one-third of the students in public schools stayed home in a district that is over fifty percent Latino. At Florida International University, the local campus of the state university system, which has a student body that is more than fifty percent Latino, about seven hundred administrative and support workers participated in the stoppage—including President Modesto Maidique, a Cuban American. At least a few businesses closed out of fear after receiving threats of bombs or boycotts. Two Hialeah businesses—Denny's and Kmart—received bomb threats for staying open. Denny's closed after the second threat. Kmart remained open, but had police sweep the store. A Winn-Dixie grocery store in a mixed but primarily Latino neighborhood was evacuated after receiving a bomb threat. Even one church had to close because of threats. St. Kieran's Catholic Church, a mostly Latino congregation in Coconut Grove, closed after the church secretary received an anonymous call saying that the church would be bombed if it stayed open.

Miami's Cuban Americans had believed that the United States supported them in their efforts to defeat Castro's communist regime. They viewed themselves as the most stalwart of all Americans in opposing communism and thus supporting U.S. interests. They further viewed themselves as strongly contributing to U.S. society both by being successful economically and through their intense civic engagement, as reflected in their high rates of naturalization and their ability to elect Cuban American officials locally. Moreover, they strongly believed that living in the United States away from one's parents was preferable to being in Cuba, even with one's parent(s). They pointed to the "successes" of the Pedro (Peter) Pan project, sponsored by the Catholic Church in the 1960s, in which Cuban parents voluntarily sent their unaccompanied children to the United States because they feared that the Cuban government would take them away and "brainwash" them. They claimed that Elián's father was under duress when he asserted that he had freely decided that he wanted Elián to return to Cuba. Given the widely documented human rights abuses of Cuba's Castro regime, they had been confident that the U.S. government would not force Elián to return to his father, and they were shocked when the INS forcibly removed Elián from his Miami relatives' home. For all these reasons, they saw the U. S. actions as a "betrayal," a breaking of the implicit contract in which they not only were staunch anti-communists but also had successfully integrated economically and politically.

The mayor of the City of Miami, Joe Carollo, condemned the INS raid and in its wake succeeded in obtaining the resignation of the non-Latino white city manager along with the police chief. Cuban Americans replaced both. The mayor of Hialeah, Raul Martinez, the most heavily Latino municipality in Miami-Dade County (and the United States), announced that Cubans should not allow themselves to be stepped on by other minorities and that they should consider forming their own political party. He asserted that Cubans had worked hard to build the community and they had nothing to apologize about. He went on to demand that the mayor of Miami-Dade County, Penelas, stand up to the black community. "The time has come to say: It's like this. How many federal programs have been put in place, how many state programs have been put in place, to help the blacks and the blacks haven't done anything. And the so-called black leaders have taken the money."

In contrast, non-Cubans viewed the Cubans as ungrateful immigrants who had been allowed to enjoy the freedoms of the United States and then attacked it by flying the U.S. flag upside down and condemning U. S. authorities who only wanted to reunite a small boy with his one surviving parent. Cheryl Lynn Conrad declared, "Janet Reno did what she had to do—uphold the law. The raid was very well executed. They were in and out very quickly with minimal risk to the child." She added that the defiance of the González family forced the hand of authorities. Others in immigrant communities took the opportunity to highlight that the INS behaves similarly in hundreds of immigration cases every year and no one takes a second look—until the victims are Cubans.

Accordingly, the strike following the raid had little economic impact outside of the Latino neighborhoods. The county's two major economic engines, Miami International Airport and the Port of Miami-Dade, remained open. While the airport saw no signs of the strike, the port slowed down, as hundreds of truck drivers stayed home. County transit buses and Metrorail operated regularly but carried fewer passengers than usual. Reportedly, only one out of ten Miami-Dade County employees stayed home. At lunchtime, the only major evidence of a strike along Ocean Drive in South Beach was the closure of Lario's on the Beach, the restaurant owned by Cuban American singer Gloria Estefan.

Nevertheless, the strike upset many non-Cubans. Potter Walker, an

African American, declared that Cuban Americans who closed their businesses were being "ungrateful to our government by not working today." The following weekend counter-demonstrations emerged in non-Latino neighborhoods. These counter-demonstrations brought together an unlikely alliance of good ole boys waving confederate flags and proudly holding signs exhorting authorities to "send them *all*" back, next to African American families reminding Mayor Penelas that "you represent us too, mayor." Within a week, flag stores in Miami claimed they were running out of both American and Cuban flags, especially the small ones that people mount on their cars. The Miami Cubans were chastised across the board by non-Latinos as ungrateful, unforgiving, and unpatriotic. "Why are they waving Cuban flags?" said a colleague from New York. "If they are so adamant that he stay here since this place is so much better, why not wave American flags?"

The Elián case even affected the 2000 election. It was an election in which African Americans in South Florida, as in the state as a whole, turned out in record numbers to vote for Al Gore, the Democratic Party candidate. It was equally an election in which Cuban Americans turned out en masse to vote against the Democrats. Ever since President Kennedy ordered the failed Bay of Pigs invasion of Cuba, Miami's Cubans have overwhelmingly voted Republican. Democratic presidential contenders have never won Miami Cubans' votes. Bill Clinton did make inroads, capturing as much as 40 percent of their votes in 1996. However, in 2000, in the wake of Elián's forcible return to Cuba, more than 80 percent of Miami Cubans voted for Bush, who won Florida, and thus the presidency, by only a few hundred votes.

Interested and disinterested observers watching these events must have asked themselves, and any who would listen: What's with Miami? What's with these Miami Cubans, perhaps America's most successful immigrant group, certainly the most successful Latinos, complaining about the U. S. government betraying them? Are they a bunch of ingrates? Some interpreted the behavior of Cubans as par for the course,

the arrogance that has characterized the most successful Latino immigrant group since the beginning of its mass arrival in the United States
in 1959. Cubans, as equal citizens of this country, should be respectful,
if not accepting, of its laws. Others, more mercifully, expressed respect
for the position of those who, even after forty years of exile, refuse to negotiate principles for popularity; those who face what they consider to
be unjust laws and declare that " the law is an ass."

America welcomed Cuban exiles when they fled Cuba in the wake of
its communist revolution. The U. S. government showered unparalleled
benefits upon them: retraining and recertification for professionals,
scholarships, travel expenses from Cuba to the U.S., permanent residence status, and business loans. They took advantage of it all. Miami
Cubans exercise political control of the City of Miami, Miami-Dade
County, and the Miami Dade County public schools. They have ample
representation in the state legislature and hold two seats in the U. S.
Congress. Moreover, they wield enormous influence over U. S. foreign
policy toward Cuba. Arguably, by 1990 it was clear that these first-generation immigrants and their children had made it in America more
quickly than any previous immigrant community in American history.

The Elián affair brought to light many of the strains of their relation
to current U. S. laws and national opinion. Those engaged in this controversy were talking, indirectly, about the dynamics of assimilation,
about how they view the process of becoming American. They were also
confronting one of the most important issues in contemporary America:
to what extent and in what ways can America absorb the current great
wave of immigration? The Elián affair encapsulates the central argument of this book: that immigrant assimilation is not just about the immigrants changing themselves and becoming American. Rather, assimilation also entails a reciprocal effect: immigrants are not assimilated
until the rest of America accepts them as part of America. In heavily immigrant communities, the threshold of acceptance might be different
than in a community where established residents predominate, but the

process is the same: each group has its take on what it means to be American, but the criteria is a negotiated one.

OUR RESEARCH PROBLEM

The core of our research question is encompassed in Woody Guthrie's 1940 song "This Land is Your Land," which serves as the title for this volume. While Woody's populist message was primarily an explicit class analysis, the core of his message is given a new ethnic dimension today, as waves of new immigrants, from Latin America and Asia rather than Europe, claim portions of this land as their own. We focus on a corner of the frontier society developing at the edge of the "gulf stream waters" and explore how diverse immigrant groups strive to make this land their land.

In the following chapters, we examine face-to-face, daily contact between immigrants and Americans in three arenas in Miami: business organizations, workers at their workplaces, and high-school students in schools. We examine not only highly successful Cubans, but also Haitians, who have encountered far more difficulties in Miami, and other Latin American immigrants. We focus not only on how established resident white Americans respond to immigrants, but also on how Miami's African American population reacts.

The predominant concern of immigration research has been immigrants' economic impact and their assimilation. Continuing the research trajectory started with the Ford Foundation's Changing Relations Project in the late 1980s,[1] we seek to shift the debate on immigrants from their economic impact and their relative levels of assimilation to the interaction between newcomers and established resident Americans. Such a focus incorporates consideration of economic impact and assimilation, but extends the debate to include the social impact on both established residents and immigrants, along with the attendant cultural friction and tension that has become part of America's historical legacy as a nation of immigrants. Miami is home to both black and white immigrants, some highly successful and some struggling to survive, and a diverse resident population that includes many who claim an immigrant heritage.

Miami is also a city that many Americans perceive as having been taken over by immigrants, and in reaction to those perceptions, the city spawned the contemporary English-only, immigrant backlash movement that reverberated throughout the United States. All these characteristics make Miami not only dynamic and exciting, but also a strategic research site. As in Miami, the wave of immigration since the mid-1960s has already affected most major urban areas in the United States. It is now beginning to filter down to smaller cities and towns, too. What Miami now confronts either already challenges or soon will challenge other cities.

This chapter describes how, within one generation, immigration has transformed Miami from a declining retirement and tourism center for North Americans into the northern capital of Latin America. The beginning of this process can be traced to January 1, 1959, the day the Cuban Revolution triumphed on the island ninety miles from U. S. shores. On that date, Cubans began their migratory waves to the Florida coast and other cities in the United States. The extraordinarily generous welcome afforded Cubans not only allowed them to achieve unparalleled rapid economic success, but also strained relationships among all groups in Miami. African Americans argue that Cubans received the fruits of the civil rights movement. Working-class white Americans frequently either fled the city or initiated a backlash, which included the English Only movement. White American business leaders expressed frustration and confusion that Cubans and other Latinos could succeed without really learning English or joining mainstream American business and civic organizations. Non-Cuban immigrants, such as Haitians and Nicaraguans, commonly feel that they are discriminated against compared to Cubans. These reactions are not unprecedented. We summarize how the reaction to and treatment of Cubans and other immigrants in Miami parallels America's long-term ambivalence towards all immigrants.

In contrast to the predominant theories of immigrant adaptation, which emphasize assimilation and economic adaptation, we argue that these theories no longer adequately conceptualize the problems occasioned by immigration in Miami. Instead, we outline our own theoretical framework, which stresses interaction between immigrants and Americans.

AMERICAN AMBIVALENCE

Americans seem always to be of two minds about immigration. Immigrants are celebrated in popular culture and myth. Moreover, the words inscribed on the Statue of Liberty are not empty rhetoric. Virtually every American is aware of their personal family ethnic heritage rooted in immigration, whether their ancestors came to pursue economic or political freedom or were forced to come as slaves. Temporal and psychological distance from one's personal immigration history, along with pride or shame, affect reactions to new immigrants. Two attitudes have revealed themselves in the public debate: open generosity versus nativism and racism. The United States has always either kept the door open or attempted to close the door, albeit with a substantial crack.

The United States is the leading country in the history of the world in terms of immigration. Between 1820 and 2000, over sixty-five million immigrants were admitted into the United States. Currently, the United States is one of the few countries in the world with an official immigration program. During the 1990s, immigration to the United States averaged nearly one million a year, a figure that exceeded the combined total for all other countries allowing immigration.

At the same time, immigrants have always provoked some degree of ethnocentric backlash. As historian John Higham (1988) has pointed out, at various times in American history, anti-immigrant sentiment has flared up, producing nativist excesses. Early English colonists disparaged French Huguenots for being French and Catholic, and the Scotch and Irish for not being really English (Jones 1960, 44). German immigrants to England's American colony evoked particularly passionate phobias. Belonging to pacifist sects, such as the Amish, many German immigrants sought seclusion from rather than assimilation to Anglo American ways. They prompted Benjamin Franklin to challenge, "Why should Pennsylvania, founded by the English, become a Colony of Aliens, who will shortly be so numerous as to Germanize us instead of Anglifying them?" (Weaver 1970, 50).

Immigrants were not, of course, the only manifestation of alterity that concerned English settlers. Colonists also feared those whom they had displaced, the Native Americans. Puritans considered Native Americans who assimilated by converting to Christianity as a potentially subversive, dangerous force and attempted to exterminate them in the 1670s (Dinnerstein, Nichols, and Reimers 1979, 5, 9). One hundred years later, the United States Constitution originally denied citizenship to Native Americans. Early Americans also considered African slaves and their descendants as inferior and incapable of assimilating into Anglo American culture.

Following the founding of the republic, the Federalists and Jeffersonian Republicans agreed that too many foreigners might drown American institutions. They disagreed, however, on which foreigners constituted the most important menace. The French Jacobins and Irish radicals most intimidated the conservative Federalists, while the Jeffersonians censured the French royalists and other aristocratic groups (Dinnerstein, Nichols, and Reimers 1979, 67). Nevertheless, the United States did not pass restrictive immigration laws until the Chinese Exclusion Act of 1882, which not only prevented Chinese from immigrating to the United States, but also made them ineligible for naturalization.

In 1911, in the midst of the greatest immigration wave in U. S. history, the United States Immigration Commission, better known as the Dillingham Commission, issued a forty-two-volume report with copious social and economic data. Considered moderate at the time, the commission nevertheless invidiously contrasted immigrants from Northern Europe with those from Eastern and Southern Europe. Eugenicists, such as Madison Grant in his *The Passing of the Great Race* (1916), argued that Anglo-Saxons, Nordics, and Teutonics should not contaminate their "racial purity" by marrying "lower types," such as Poles, Italians, and Greeks. Grant and his contemporaries conceived of each of these European regional groups (for example, Nordics) as fundamentally different. With the advent of World War I, fear focused on German immigrants—not on their racial purity, but on the more immediate political question of whether they were loyal to America or to Germany. Long before the multicultural wars of the 1980s and 1990s, the *Literary Digest*, one of the most important periodicals of the time, declared in 1915 that the "hyphenate issue" was the most vital one of the day. For example, presidents Theodore Roosevelt and Woodrow Wilson both asserted that German Americans had to become either Germans or Americans (Higham 1988, 198). Politicians such as Frank Houx, governor of Wyoming, asserted, "We are 100 per cent American in the State of Wyoming, and we are going to remain 100 per cent American" (Higham 1988, 194).

This climate gave birth to the anti-immigration agitation of the 1920s, the high-water mark in the history of American nativism. On May 26, 1924, the first permanent limitation on immigration was enacted in the form of the nationality origins quota system (U. S. Immigration and Naturalization Service, 1997, A.1–24). Intended to keep out Jews, Italians, Slavs, and other "undesirable" immigrants, the law succeeded. Tragically, the law later made it difficult or impossible for many Jews and others fleeing the Nazi genocide to enter the United States. The Great Depression also depressed immigration. Since most immigrants were labor migrants, a decline in employment opportunities reduced the demand for immigrant labor. The restrictive immigration laws, followed by the Great Depression, combined to reduce immigration until well after World War II. Accordingly, public concern over the adaptation and assimilation of immigrants receded.

The end of Word War II initiated prolonged economic prosperity. The Slavs and other new immigrants, supposedly essentially different from earlier immigrants, had evidently lost their distinctiveness and become white Americans. The Civil Rights movement also affected attitudes toward other groups. The blatant racism of the early twentieth century diminished. In 1965, Congress reformed the restrictive immigration law by repealing the old quotas, thus allowing for much more diversity among immigrants. In 1995, immigrants to the United States came from more than a hundred different countries, and concerns over the impact of immigration have reemerged. To many, immigrants again constitute a threat to the integrity of the United States and its cultural identity. Some observers worry not about immigration per se but about the multiculturalist turn that immigration may reinforce, which they fear may lead to national fragmentation. The historian Arthur Schlesinger Jr. asserts, "The American Creed envisages a nation composed of individuals making their own choices and accountable to themselves, not a nation based on inviolable ethnic communities" (Schlesinger 1992). A more frankly ethnocentric reaction to the new immigration is contained in a recent bestseller, wherein the English immigrant Peter Brimelow asserts that recent immigration is likely to "transform and ultimately, perhaps, even to destroy . . . the American nation" (1995, xv). The racial fears of the early twentieth century have been transformed into cultural fears.

And yet, Americans have hardly uniformly disparaged and vilified immigrants. Many observers have viewed the impact of aliens positively. As early as 1782, the French immigrant Michel Guillaume Jean de Crèvecoeur claimed, "Here individuals of all nations are melted into a new race of men, whose labors and posterity will one day cause great changes in the world" (Crèvecoeur 1782, 54–55). One hundred years ago, as America confronted its largest ever influx of new immigrants, nearly all of whom were not of British origin, the Carnegie Corporation commissioned the department of sociology at the University of Chicago to produce a series entitled *Studies of Methods of Americanization* (Kivisto 1990). The study concluded that the prospects for assimilation were good in the United States because, unlike Europe, there were no classes in the new country and immigrants arrived as individuals, not as groups. The famous American immigration phrase, the melting pot, comes from Israel Zangwill's 1908 play of that title, which states, "The Real American has not yet arrived. . . . He will be the fusion of all races, perhaps the coming superman (Zangwill 1921, 33; quoted in Parillo 1994, 12).

In the current debate, for every text denigrating immigration, such as Roy Beck's *The Case Against Immigration* (1996), there is a counter, such as Sanford J. Ungar's *Fresh Blood* (1995), which emphasizes the positive contributions of America's new immigrants. Even within the Republican Party, the strongest political hope of the anti-immigration camp, views are divided. Anti-immigrant and immigration restriction proposals almost invariably originate in Republican ranks. Nevertheless, some key Republican leaders, most notably George W. Bush, are advocates of continued immigration. Similarly, Rudolph Giuliani, the Republican mayor of New York City, unabashedly championed restoring government benefits to legal immigrants.

In short, America both welcomes and rejects immigrants. We champion our history of immigration both rhetorically and pragmatically. Politicians and others repeatedly remind us that we all (except for American Indians) are of immigrant stock, and we continue to receive more immigrants than any other nation. At the same time, many commentators, politicians, and others express fears that today's immigrants cannot assimilate, that they cannot or will not become Americans, that they will undermine America's culture, values, and institutions. Social scientists interested in immigration have devoted most of their attention to precisely this question of assimilation.

THE DOMINANT THEORY: ASSIMILATION

Assimilation became the academic term for the popular phrase "the melting pot." Amidst the last great wave of massive immigration to the United States, from the end of the nineteenth century through the restrictive laws of the 1920s, when popular opinion demanded the closure of U. S. borders, two sociologists, Robert Park and Ernest Burgess, argued that a natural process of assimilation would ease conflict and integrate immigrants. In the original academic formulation of the argument, Park and Burgess (1921) contended that there was a universal cycle of race relations that began with conflict and progressed through competition and accommodation to end in assimilation, the intergroup mixing and sharing of experiences that would induce the replacement of immigrants' ethnic or minority identity with an American temperament. Their focus was on the interaction between groups and the apparently inevitable outcome of assimilation, a comprehensive loss of immigrant identity, and the assumption of American ways, a basically one-way street.

Park and Burgess contributed to the foundation of the Chicago School, which intellectually confronted the challenge of immigrants who had been flooding into Chicago and other major American cities. Through the application of the tools of the relatively new field of sociology, they contested the then dominant view that asserted that immigrants were inherently inferior and detrimental to America. By combining direct empirical observation with analytical generalization, they redirected emphasis to the social and psychological adaptation of immigrant groups. In the process, they established many terms, such as assimilation, that have reverberated through countless other investigations and that continue to guide analysis of immigrants today. Park and Burgess attributed a central role to the interaction between immigrants and Americans through their cycle of race relations: conflict, competition, accommodation, and eventually assimilation. Subsequent research, however, shifted emphasis to the individual actions of immigrants.

The intellectual trajectory established by Park and Burgess culminated in Milton Gordon's *Assimilation in American Life: The Role of Race, Religion, and National Origins* (Gordon 1964). Following Park and Burgess and their successors, Gordon viewed assimilation as the expected outcome, a natural consequence of the immigrant experience in America. He depicted two stages: (1) Acculturation, in which immigrants shed their native language and view of the world, replacing them with English and an American cultural outlook. In Gordon's view, acculturation was a necessary precondition for the second stage. (2) Social assimilation incorporates substages of first interacting with established resident Americans and then having them as friends, close associates, and eventually marriage partners. Classical assimilation theory's assumption that acculturation precedes social assimilation corresponds closely with popular American expectations of immigrant progress. It supports the calls for English Only, which views maintenance of a foreign language as an impediment to assimilation.

Gordon's formulation also reflected a profound shift from Park and Burgess. Interaction between immigrants and established residents faded from view. Gordon emphasized the individual immigrants as the prime movers in assimilation. From his perspective, individuals separately assimilated and the sum of individuals' actions produced assimilation of immigrant groups. Gordon's analysis conformed well with the experiences of the immigrant flows from Europe in the late nineteenth and early twentieth centuries, whose second- and third-generation offspring had apparently assimilated by the late 1950s and early 1960s, when Gordon's work appeared. The 1960s, however, saw an ethnic resurgence, most obviously by African Americans in the civil rights struggle, but also by numerous hyphenated white Americans. Glazer and Moynihan (1970) described the "unmeltable ethnics," such as Italians in New York, who maintained their distinctiveness and separation. Yet, subsequent research demonstrated more melting than Glazer and Moynihan apparently saw (Alba and Nee 1997).

The ethnicity of white ethnics was typically more symbolic than fundamental. They did recognize their foreign roots and ate distinctive national foods. However, their ethnic expressions were usually limited to special occasions and to foods that had been absorbed into American cuisine. In contrast, those whom Americans defined as racially different—blacks, Latinos, and Asians—were more likely not only to maintain symbolic ethnicity but also to experience difficulty in being accepted by and assimilating into mainstream, established-resident white American society. As the color of immigration changed, the apparent problem of assimilating immigrants reemerged and presented far stronger challenges to the standard views of assimilation.

In 1965, changes in immigration law brought many more, and mainly non-European, primarily Latino and Asian, immigrants to the United States. Academic attention has centered on whether immigrants are succeeding economically and on the economic impact their presence has on the United States.[2] The 1997 National Academy of Sciences report, for example, fixes exclusively on assessing the economic impact of immigrants. This report concludes that the economic effect of contemporary immigrants is positive overall for the nation, but it also admits that local governments shoulder an immediate burden in the areas of the cost of schooling and health care for low-wage immigrant workers and their families. In cities where low-skilled immigrants and minorities are concentrated, the report also concludes that they compete with each other for jobs.

The National Academy of Science report reflects end-of-the-century policy debates that often focus on the cost-benefit ratio of immigration. Recent changes in policy, including certain provisions of welfare reform (the Personal Responsibility and Work Opportunity Reconciliation Act of 1996) and the 1996 Immigration Act (the Illegal Immigration Reform and Immigrant Responsibility Act of 1996) reflect the desire to curtail the net cost of immigration through limiting immigrant access to benefits and services and/or transferring some of the costs to the immigrants themselves or their countries of origin. Welfare reform, for example, originally eliminated food stamps and supplemental security income (SSI, which goes to disabled and elderly individuals) for adult legal immigrants, although these provisions were reversed about a year later. The 1996 Immigration Act expanded the basis for denying immigrant visas to persons deemed likely to become a public charge by considering factors such as age, health, family status, financial resources, education, and skills.

These policy initiatives and their associated, although usually implicit, theoretical perspectives miss the issues raised by the Elián affair, discussed at the beginning of this chapter. The economic adaptation and impact of immigrants are important, but they are not the only significant features of immigration. The fact that immigrants succeed economically does not mean that Americans will accept them. Moreover, the new immigrants can succeed economically without first acculturating. Heavy Spanish accents come from the most successful as well as struggling immigrants. Miami is different from Chicago in the 1920s. Immigrants succeed economically without acculturating, yet they still confront prejudice and discrimination. Economics cannot capture the full story of the impact of immigrants, especially in a place like Miami, where immigrants insist on taking Woody at his word.

MIAMI: CAPITAL OF LATIN AMERICA

At a 1998 event held by the University of Miami and the state of Florida to discuss plans for educating a "multilingual workforce for the twenty-first century," the university's newly installed dean of education, an import from a university in the north, spoke of language diversity as a problem that people in his former area of residence would soon be encountering. The faculty member moderating the conference gently reminded the dean that in Florida multilingualism is viewed as an asset, and promised to continue to educate him.

In Miami, multilingualism is an asset. Not only are Latinos the demographic majority, but they also have considerable economic and political power. Latinos are the majority in some Texas cities, such as Laredo, El Paso, and San Antonio, and in border areas, such as California's Imperial Valley, but there they lack the clout they have in Miami. It is easier to find a job, to shop, just to get things done, if one knows Spanish. It is also much easier to advance economically if one knows English. Miami is truly multilingual and multicultural (Garreau 1981; Levine 1985; Portes and Stepick 1993).[3]

Miami has many foreigners, almost all with roots in Latin America and the Caribbean, and its economic focus is on Latin America and the Caribbean. Miami has the highest proportion of foreign-born residents of any major metropolitan area in the United States, proportionally 50 percent more than either Los Angeles or New York. Over 70 percent of Miami's population are either first-generation (48.6 percent) or second-generation (22.9 percent) immigrants (Portes and Rumbaut 2001).[4] In the 1980s, Latinos achieved a plurality, and by the early 1990s an absolute majority, of the population in Miami-Dade County. By the 2000 census, Miami-Dade County was nearly 60 percent Latino. With about 600,000 Cubans, Miami-Dade County contains the largest concentration of Cubans in the United States, and Cubans have always constituted a majority of the local Latino population. Beginning in the 1980s, other Latino immigrants also began settling in the Miami area. Nicaraguans, first fleeing the Sandinista regime and then the Contra war against the Sandinistas, made Miami the largest Nicaraguan settlement in the United States with over 100,000 people. In the wake of every crisis in Latin America, the Miami Latino population grows. In the 1990s, Colombians fleeing the drug wars took up residence in Miami. In the late 1990s, Peruvians and Venezuelans sought refuge from political uncertainty. With these continuing influxes, Miami's Latino population continues to grow both absolutely and proportionately (Boswell 1994; Viglucci, Yardley, and Henderson 2001). By 2000, Latinos had even become the largest minority statewide, surpassing blacks (Viglucci, Driscoll, and Henderson 2001).[5]

But it is not just the number of foreigners that makes Miami the de facto capital of Latin America. Even more important is what Latinos are doing in Miami. Miami's Latinos have made Miami the economic and transportation gateway of the Americas. While Miami has only five percent of the total U. S. Latino population, it has close to half of the forty largest Latino-owned industrial and commercial firms in the country. Only New York has more foreign-owned banks than Miami. Nearly 50 percent of U. S. exports to the Caribbean and Central America and over 30 percent of U. S. exports to South America pass through Miami. Miami's Free Trade Zone is the first and largest privately owned trade zone in the world. Miami's airport is the top U. S. airport for international freight, with more nonstop cargo flights to Latin America and the Caribbean than Orlando, Houston, New Orleans, Atlanta, Tampa, and New York's Kennedy Airport combined. The airport also has more airlines than any other airport in the Western Hemisphere, and it is frequently easier to get from one Latin American country to another by going through Miami than by flying direct. Miami also has the largest cruise port in the world, transporting primarily U. S. passengers on vacations throughout the Caribbean and Latin America while many of the citizens of those same countries are immigrating to Miami. While Miami may not be a global city equal to New York or London, it is assuredly the economic capital of Latin America (Nijman 1996a; Nijman 1996b; Nijman 1996c; Nijman 1997), and its Latino immigrants made it so.

The influence of Miami's Latinos extends beyond economics into politics. In 1983, Latinos captured a majority in Hialeah, the county's second-largest city. The Miami City Commission turned majority Cuban American in 1985 and has had a Cuban American mayor almost continually since then.[6] In 1996, Alex Penelas became the county's first Cuban American mayor. In addition, by 1998, the County Commission achieved a Cuban American majority. The City Commission of Miami Beach, the county's third largest city, became majority Cuban American in the fall of 1999. Two Miami Cubans are in the U. S. House of Representatives, and the Miami-Dade County state legislative delegation along with the Miami-Dade County School Board are dominated by foreign-born Latinos, specifically Cubans. Many of the area's most important private firms are headed by Latinos, including Miami Cubans. The largest Latino firm in the country, MasTec Telecom, is based in Miami. Miami also has the largest Latino real estate development company in the United States, the largest Latino-owned banks, and the majority of construction firms in the county. Latino representatives of the real estate and construction industries have become the movers and shakers in local politics. Miami-Dade Community College has more foreign students, mostly Latino, than any other college or university in the nation. The overall ratings of one of the three Spanish-language local television stations are higher than those of any of the local English-language television stations. Not only is the majority foreign-born, but also it firmly retains its Latino culture. Not only do the gardeners and busboys speak Spanish, but so do those who own the houses and patronize the upscale restaurants. One of the Miami-Dade County School Board members speaks English with such a heavy accent that native speakers of English complain they cannot understand him. Yet, these unacculturated Latinos have risen quickly. Indeed, never before in U. S. history has a first-generation immigrant group achieved such power in a major U. S. city.

Miami's immigrants are not all Latinos. Miami also has had a significant influx of Caribbean, primarily black, immigrants (Dunn 1997). Much of the original Black population that settled and built Miami at the end of the nineteenth century was from the Bahamas (George 1978; Mohl 1987a). Many Miami blacks who appear as African Americans to outsiders claim a distinctively Bahamian background. More recently, other Caribbean blacks have settled in Miami. Florida's Haitian population in the 2000 census was nearly 270,000, making it the largest in the United States, surpassing the number of Haitians in the New York metropolitan area.[7] Jamaicans in Florida number almost 170,000. All of the growth in the black population in Miami-Dade County between 1980 and 2000 came from black immigration.

All these immigrants settled in an area in which few established resident Americans have deep roots. One hundred years ago, south Florida was isolated and unbearably hot and humid, with few people for the vast swarms of mosquitoes. The opening of the railroad in 1896 initiated links to the northern United States, which permitted the export of fruits and winter vegetables and the import of tourists and retirees. Miami grew primarily through Americans migrating southward, especially after the advent of air conditioning. White Americans relocated primarily from the Northeast and Midwest, and included many Jews. Through the 1970s, Miami had the largest Jewish concentration in the United States outside of New York City, and through the 1990s it had the largest concentration of holocaust survivors. Beginning in the 1970s, however, the number of white Americans in Miami (more specifically, non-Latino whites) began to decline as many moved out of Miami-Dade County. By 2000, they constituted barely over 20 percent of the region, considerably less than the nearly 60 percent Latino population and only slightly more than the black population.

Nevertheless, established resident whites maintained control beyond their numbers. The leaders of businesses with the most employees in Miami-Dade are 60 percent white. Seventy-five percent of Miami-Dade County judges are white. And in the county's major arts organizations, they constitute 89 percent of the leadership. Even on college and university boards and in political posts, white non-Latinos hold more than half of the positions (Branch-Brioso 2000a). While a large independent Spanish-language newspaper has long been based in Miami *(Diaro las Americas)*, the most influential newspaper, the *Miami Herald*, is controlled by established resident whites. Even in elected positions, Latinos lag behind whites. A 2000 *Miami Herald* survey of 406 government positions found that whites held 51 percent of elected and top appointed jobs, while Latinos only had 32 percent (all but 5 percent were Miami Cubans; Branch-Brioso 2000a). Consistent with continued power and influence, established resident white professionals and executives have kept on migrating into Miami from other parts of the United States at the same time as working-class whites are abandoning the area. The Jewish population in Miami began declining as early as the mid-1960s (Moore 1994; Rudavsky 2000), and the established resident white population started dropping in absolute numbers in the mid-1970s. The number of established resident whites has declined ever since. After Hurricane Andrew in 1992, emigration of whites increased even more (Yardley and Grotto 2001). Yet throughout this period, white professionals and executives have still been relocating in Miami. By the year 2000, the only areas in Miami-Dade County with a majority non-Hispanic white population were three affluent neighborhoods bordering Biscayne Bay.

Miami's African American population was more likely to have come from other regions of the South, such as northern Florida, Georgia, and Alabama (Dunn 1997). Their proportion of the population was consistently around 20 percent throughout the twentieth century. As black immigration increased in the 1980s, however, the proportion of African Americans declined. Since the 1980s, at least 25 percent of Miami's black population has been foreign-born (Boswell 1994) and of the 75 percent who are U. S.-born, a significant number still recognize a Caribbean heritage.

Miami's race relations have been undeniably southern. Until the civil rights movement at the middle of the twentieth century, Miami politics excluded blacks. Segregation was officially sanctioned, and brutality against blacks was not unknown (Mohl 1987a; Dunn 1997). Since the beginning of significant immigration in the 1960s, Miami has experienced repeated urban unrest, with major riots occurring four times in the ten years from 1980 to 1990 (Porter and Dunn 1984; Dunn 1997). Police actions provoked each riot, and the local media interpreted them all as part of the general American story of race relations, that is, blacks responding to white police brutality. However, they also carried an undercurrent of tensions caused by immigration. In one riot, the primary participants were black Puerto Ricans. In another, a Colombian-born policeman shot and killed a Caribbean black. Moreover, since the 1960s, local African Americans have frequently expressed frustration that the gains of Miami Cubans have come at their expense, that Miami Cubans are just as racist—if not more so—than white Americans. African Americans and Haitians have repeatedly formed a united front against what they perceive as the racial discrimination in immigration policy that favors white Cubans over black Haitians.

Miami's relatively rapid transformation into the capital of Latin

America confuses, frustrates, and frequently alienates both established resident Americans and Miami's immigrants. Latino immigrants who do not speak English feel that established resident Americans do not understand that it is difficult to learn another language, especially when low-wage jobs mean long hours in the company of other Latino immigrants. Bilingual Latinos think that White and Black Americans arrogantly fail to appreciate the value of knowing more than one language and do not respect Latinos for their bilingualism. Established resident Americans, when confronted with the growing number of recent immigrants who do not speak English, often conclude that it is in part because today's immigrants do not want to learn English or that they fail to appreciate the importance of English in the United States. They worry about ethnic balkanization or simply feel irritated about "feeling foreign in my own land." Such cultural issues animate immigration and language restrictionists' anxiety that America is becoming an "alien nation."[8]

As immigration from Latin America continues, the situation in Miami is likely to foretell changes and challenges throughout the United States. Moreover, because Latinization has so thoroughly transformed the region, Miami presents a theoretically important case of immigrants successfully challenging the power structure of established resident Americans. Many of Miami's immigrants are different from former peasants and low-wage, unskilled workers who hope that their children can make it in America. Rather, many of Miami's first-generation immigrants arrived with significant levels of education and skills and have already succeeded. They have discovered that rather than ensuring complete assimilation, political and economic success may evoke American ambivalence and even rejection.

REFOCUSING ON RELATIONSHIPS

For an immigrant to assimilate, to become an American, he or she must receive respect and acceptance from the rest of America, from the established residents. Similarly, whether an immigrant group becomes accepted does not depend solely on what the immigrants say or do. Rather, it unfolds from the interaction between immigrants and established resident Americans, those who were born and raised in the United States, who view themselves as the real or mainstream Americans.

In this book, we reestablish interaction between immigrants and established residents as a central focus, as the fulcrum for not only cultural struggles but also assimilation. Contrary to Park and Burgess, however, we do not argue that interactions progress through a natural, inevitable, and universal cycle from conflict through competition, accommodation, and eventually assimilation. Our research reveals that interaction sometimes proceeds relatively smoothly and at other times it is suffused with tension. Sometimes it is a process that produces individuals who appear to be mainstream Americans, and other times marginalized minorities emerge. Sometimes individuals and groups lose their distinctive cultural traits; at times native culture is expressed primarily in private in one's home or among one's co-ethnics; and for some, native culture endures, permeates, and alters established residents' American culture. Instead of reflecting individual immigrants' beliefs and actions, we argue that the quality and form of interaction depends upon the relative power of groups within a particular context.

While the Chicago School developed its paradigms by portraying immigrants from the point of view of established American society, the Miami perspective looks at the issue from the perspective of the immigrant groups, as well as the natives. In Miami, both the immigrants and the established resident Americans have changed, while not becoming the same. Based upon our research and experience in Miami, we intend to delineate the forces behind this variation and the specific contexts in which different expressions and outcomes occur by exploring three variables previously ignored in assimilation studies: power, context, and diversity.

By power, we mean the ability to control or influence others' behavior. During the great wave of migration at the beginning of the twentieth century, power relationships were unquestioned. English-speaking

White Americans dominated, and thus controlled the nature of relationships and associated paths of assimilation. Big-city public schools were English-only, although in some rural areas school was taught in languages other than English, with, for example, German schools being common in Wisconsin (Piore 1979; Glazer 1993). Overall and especially in America's cities, immigrants were expected to speak English and only English in order to be accepted by Americans. The railroads, steel manufacturers, and stockyards all employed immigrants, but the owners and managers conducted business in English. Similarly, while immigrants gained influence in local politics through big-city machines such as Tammany Hall, their representatives in local government, state legislatures, and the U. S. Congress all spoke English as their first language. It seemed obvious that Americans set the rules of interaction and assimilation. To succeed, immigrants had to become Americans, learn the ropes using English, and only then gain acceptance and access to American-dominated institutions.

Now, at least in some locations, things have changed. Cubans have a power seldom achieved by first-generation immigrants. By the early 1990s, just thirty years after Cubans began arriving, they controlled the most important local political machinery and they had deeply penetrated the most important economic arenas. Some aspects of Cuban power are obvious, such as their representation in Miami's electoral politics and their impact on Miami-Dade County Public Schools (MD-CPS). In contrast to the anti-bilingual policies instituted in California in 1998, MDCPS forcefully endorsed and advanced bilingual education. Every child is encouraged to become bilingual. Native English speakers are expected to take Spanish through elementary school.

Less visible power that we describe in subsequent chapters includes forceful efforts by mainstream Miami business organizations to recruit Miami Cuban businesspeople. It also includes the participation of Miami Cuban workers in an apparel plant's success at undermining American management practices. The power of the immigrants makes a difference both in relationships and in the path of assimilation. Americans cannot ignore Miami's Cubans and other Miami Latinos and assume the newcomers will become just like mainstream Americans. The Latino newcomers have less urgency to learn English, and there is a greater presence of Spanish and other aspects of Latino culture. Americans now have to adapt to the immigrants at the same time as the immigrants adapt to America.

Yet Miami Cuban power is more limited in other arenas. As chapter two will demonstrate, American business and civic leaders have vacillated and struggled with how to respond to the growth of the Cuban and Latino population. In spite of Latino economic clout, the largest private firms, such as the utilities and tourist industries, are still controlled by White Americans. Moreover, many Miami Cubans still feel as if they have not been completely accepted, they have not completely assimilated into the local society, feelings confirmed by the Elián affair. At the beginning of the new century, Miami Cubans debate whether they need to have a separate voice as "Cubans," or more generally as "Hispanics," or whether they should continue the struggle individually within the framework of mainstream institutions. Their power provides them with a voice, but it does not imply either assimilation or full equality, or even access to all arenas.

The American business and civic elite must negotiate with Miami Cuban business and political leaders. Through the 1980s and into the 1990s, Latino newcomers and established resident businesspeople came to realize that they share a profound interest in promoting and protecting a good business environment in Miami. Newcomers and established residents do not always define this interest exactly alike, but business and community organizations provide a context in which each informs and influences the other.

The gradual transformation of relationships leads us to strongly emphasize that relationships are very much processual. From year to year, week to week, and even day to day, relationships between groups change dramatically. Moreover, relationships do not inevitably progress as Park and Burgess described, that is, from competition toward assimilation.

Relationships between Miami's Cubans and established resident White Americans have experienced innumerable forward and backward steps. As described in an earlier work (Portes and Stepick 1993), until 1980 many Miami Cubans thought they had assimilated, that Americans had accepted them. But the sudden influx of over 125,000 Cubans from the Cuban port of Mariel in 1980 created a vehement backlash against all Cubans, dramatically reversing the apparent good relations of Miami's Cubans and Americans. In the 1990s, many Miami Cubans assumed that they had gained control of their destiny, that their will would be the way, at least locally. The Elián affair revealed the limits on their power and the resentment that others held toward them.

Because of the variation in relationships across contexts, we have chosen arenas as our unit of analysis. We conceive of arenas as fields of social relations that contain significant social interaction between newcomers and established residents. There are numerous arenas in Miami where newcomers and established residents interact face-to-face on a daily basis. In Miami, we selected three institutional arenas: the work place, schools, and business and commerce. These embraced interaction among all of Miami's main groups: established resident blacks and whites, Cubans and other Latino newcomers, and Haitian newcomers.

METHODOLOGY AND
STRUCTURE OF THE BOOK

Much public debate is based upon armchair observations: reading of the media and other sources removed from the face-to-face interactions of everyday life, such as the data from the Immigration and Naturalization Service and the U.S. Census. We base our analysis, in contrast, on more than a decade of systematic, intensive, direct observation of how people actually get along on a day-to-day, face-to-face basis. Moreover, each of us has lived in Miami for more than fifteen years, spending nearly all that time intimately involved in living through and analyzing immigrant and established resident interactions. Not only have we engaged in research, but each of us has been involved in numerous community organizations. Specifically, this book began as the Miami component of a project sponsored by the Ford Foundation, *Changing Relations Between Newcomers and Established Residents*. That larger project took place in six cities: Philadelphia (Goode and Schneider 1994), Chicago (Conquergood 1992), Monterey Park in the greater Los Angeles area (Horton 1995), Houston (Hagan 1994), and Garden City, Kansas (Stull, Broadway, and Erickson1992), and Miami. It was designed specifically as an anthropological examination of the actual state of relations between newcomers and established residents.

The fundamental methodology of the research was participant observation complemented by intensive interviewing. In each arena, our general approach was to first do some open-ended interviews, usually with gatekeepers to whom we had to explain our project in order to gain access. We usually exploited that opportunity to ask questions about relationships and generally obtained positive evaluations of these. If one were to rely solely on formal interviews concerning relationships between newcomers and established residents in Miami, two contradictory images would emerge. On the one hand, those who represent important local institutions (such as the chamber of commerce or school principals) articulate a "can do" approach, usually avoiding the language of conflict. Diversity, in this approach, is positive, and conflict can be managed. Others, particularly those who have little power and are in positions that are inherently competitive (such as apparel workers) often relate highly negative stereotypes of other groups and blame these other groups (who could be either newcomers or established residents) as the source of Miami's problems, or at least those problems in a particular arena.

The subsequent participant observation provided numerous concrete examples that often contradicted the original interviews and provided guides to later intensive interviews, which were done toward the end of the research. At the work sites, the combination of participant observation among workers and interviews with managers revealed differences within the organization, as top-level managers glossed over established resident-newcomer differences, while floor supervisors emphasized established resident-newcomer conflict. Participant observation revealed that established resident-newcomer and Black-White conflict are undeniably present but largely controlled by the nature of the work and unwritten work culture. Other examples of the contradictions between the interviews and participant observation are discussed in the Methodological Appendix, where we also indicate who did which parts of the fieldwork. While all of this book's authors conducted fieldwork, we also incorporated graduate students, without whom this work could not have been accomplished. We would specifically like to thank Peggy Nolan, Hafidh M. Hafidh, and Steve Morris, along with Aline LaBorwit, Eddie Compas, Debbie Draznin, and Bernadette Copée. While we do not claim to know, let alone present, all aspects of immigrant and established resident relationships, we do believe that we have a firsthand, empirically-based perspective that reflects ongoing processes. The Methodological Appendix details our methodology and provides details of the broader project of which this research is a part.

Chapter two addresses the business arena. Because of the extraordinary economic success in Miami's Latino community, the arena of business assumes great importance in Miami. Nowhere else have first-generation Latino entrepreneurs been so successful, and nowhere else have established resident White business leaders felt so compelled to incorporate Latinos into business organizations. The business arena contains primarily interaction between established resident Whites and newcomer Miami Cubans. It provides an important complement to the more common focus on working-class immigrants. Specifically, it results in what we have termed reverse acculturation, when established residents self-consciously adopt some traits of the newcomer culture, in particular, learning Spanish and promoting Miami as the capital of Latin America.

Chapter three discusses interaction at the workplace. Most immigration, both historically and contemporarily, is labor migration, that is, immigrants who come looking for and expecting to work. For adult newcomers, Americanization occurs primarily in the workplace. We selected three different kinds of workplaces: a large construction site, an apparel plant, and two hotels with restaurants. All of these work sites have incorporated significant numbers of immigrants both in Miami and the rest of the United States. While most immigrants are labor migrants, few studies focus specifically on the impact that the workplace has. For immigrants to Miami, the workplace makes a huge difference, with workers in a unionized construction site assimilating a class-conscious perspective, workers in an apparel plant relying upon their Latino solidarity to resist what was to them a cold-hearted, American, bureaucratized reorganization, and workers in hotels and restaurants being fragmented from each other.

Chapter four presents our results from the schools. We selected schools because they have historically played a critical role in the process of Americanization. Moreover, Miami-Dade County Public Schools (MDCPS) led the nation in the 1960s in introducing bilingual education. MDCPS is the fourth largest school district in the nation (after New York, Los Angeles, and Chicago). But unlike these other urban areas, where growth was acquired gradually, the MDCPS has grown more than 33 percent during the 1990s. It incorporates more than 13,000 new students every year and is chronically and acutely overcrowded. Slightly over one-half of MDCPS students are Latinos (or what MDCPS calls Hispanics), and about one-third are black (or non-Hispanic black). The MDCPS figures, however, do not distinguish among different nationalities. MDCPS does not know what proportion of the black population identifies as Bahamian, Haitian, or West Indian, versus African American. The school where we focused most of our attention contained primarily interaction between African Americans and Haitians, two groups who came into only limited contact in our other two arenas, business and the workplace. Interactions between black immigrants and African Americans are relatively understudied, as the traditional literature focuses on non-Black immigrants. More recent literature examines Latino and Asian immigrants. There is some literature on the interactions between African Americans and Asians or Latinos, but virtually none that addresses African American and black immigrants. Important exceptions include Woldemikael 1989; Kasinitz 1992; Waters 1994; Waters 1999. At least one theoretical article argues that the assimilation of black immigrants differs fundamentally from that of white immigrants (Portes and Zhou 1993; Portes and Zhou 1994). Our examination of Haitian-African American interactions in the schools will indicate how critical race is for black immigrants.

We conclude in chapter five by returning to the theoretical issues introduced in this chapter to assess what difference it makes to come from a different country (for instance, Cuba versus Haiti), how power influences interactions, the complications of diversity, and the role of race. We conclude that while immigration does appear to inevitably induce some conflict, things can be much better. We indicate how perceptions can be more powerful than reality, how conflict occurs just as easily over cultural as economic matters, and that social class makes a difference in who is likely to come into conflict and who is likely to make accommodations. Finally, we suggest some ways to improve relations between newcomers and established residents, which include not only treating newcomers equally, but also encouraging ethnic-specific events and events that bring everyone together. We conclude that the multicultural wars fundamentally miss the mark in arguing that either one should promote ethnic culture or a common American culture.

TWO

Competing Elites

Cuban Power, Anglo Conversion, and Frustrated African Americans

Francena Thomas, an African American middle-level administrator in county government, was not interested in insulting people; she tried to frame her criticism constructively. It was, after all, a meeting called by the Community Relations Board, and she knew many of the American whites and Latinos there. The issue was power and how the Cubans exercised it. "Sometimes you act like a nine-hundred-pound gorilla," she proclaimed. Guillermo Martinez, a Cuban journalist, later a member of the editorial board of the *Miami Herald*, admitted, "That's true, but you should realize one thing. What you are seeing now is a nine-hundred-pound *baby* gorilla."

By the year 2000, the baby gorilla had grown up, although debate continued on whether it had matured. Just about everyone in Miami was convinced that Miami's Cubans had taken over. A poll by the *Miami Herald* indicated that at least 80 percent of American whites and blacks, along with 63 percent of Miami Cubans, believed Miami Cubans controlled local politics (Branch-Brioso 2000b). As mentioned in chapter one, Miami's Cubans do exercise unprecedented sway locally. But their power did not come naturally or easily. Until the late 1980s, American white leaders kept waiting for Miami's Cubans to assimilate, to become like them so that the newcomer Cubans could then be gradually admitted to the organizations and committees that exercised local power and influence.

TWO CHALLENGES: INCORPORATING CUBANS, BARGAINING WITH BLACKS

For the last two decades of the twentieth century, Miami's American white corporate elite faced two daunting challenges: .

1. Immigrants were increasingly carving out ever-larger slices of political power. Latinos' political presence combined with their economic and cultural ascendancy challenged the corporate leaders' earlier hegemony in setting the local agenda. While some concluded that Latinos were not significantly different, at least once assimilated, others were convinced that assimilation was unlikely or too slow. Something had to be done about that nine-hundred-pound gorilla.

2. At the same time, frustration and anger ran especially high in the city's impoverished African American community. Through the 1980s and 1990s, Miami had more violent racial disturbances than any other urban area in America, and this was not good for Miami's most visible industry, tourism. Moreover, the issues of race and immigration intertwined and often appeared inseparable, as well as intractable. Miami's African and white Americans commonly felt that Miami's Cuban successes had come at the expense of black progress.

The business leadership group confronted with these twin challenges was of relatively recent origin and had come together to address a different set of problems, mainly reversing urban decline and promoting growth and development. Into the 1950s and early 1960s, Miami was essentially a southern city, albeit one with a large Jewish presence and an eye to the Caribbean. Few local leaders had roots generations deep in South Florida. Seemingly, everyone had come from somewhere else, at least everyone who was a leader. Some had migrated from the Old

South. Others had come from Cleveland, Pittsburgh, or Chicago. Many had grown up in New York. Miami, and especially Miami Beach, had become a center of American Jewish life (second only to New York City in population), the home of Israel bonds, and the site of an Israeli consulate (Moore 1994). All of them came to Miami because it was a new frontier, a growing tourist town becoming an international city. But like every new, frontier town, everything was unsettled. There was no Tammany Hall or good ole boys network. Business and political groups and organizations certainly existed, but support and membership were more diffuse than in older cities.

Of course, life went on and things got done, at least some things. The Orange Bowl had its yearly extravaganza. Leaders played golf, went fishing, and made money. For many, that was sufficient. But the laid-back attitude worried and frustrated others. They worried that problems were accumulating, that no single, unified voice was addressing the future, and that the diffused leadership was inefficient. A business leader who came to Miami in the 1960s recalls:

> I found myself initially plunged into the battle of fighting to get
> community organizations to be more reflective of this community,
> looking at it from the Jewish issue and the black issue—such things
> as the Orange Bowl Committee membership, black high-school
> bands, private clubs that discriminated, membership in community
> organizations. Those were battles I felt should have been dealt with
> years ago and I was immediately plunged into considerable contro-
> versy over some of those issues. The response I got when I attacked
> these things, I met resistance. There were strong feelings.

Alvah Chapman, then an executive with Knight-Ridder, a communications company whose flagship is the *Miami Herald*, was the key figure in convoking and organizing corporate elites to develop and push through a more progressive agenda for the city's future. Before Chapman assumed the chairmanship of the Greater Miami Chamber of Commerce (GMCC), the organization was struggling on the brink of bankruptcy. The ineffectiveness of the chamber in particular and the city's business leadership in general appalled Chapman. He attacked the problem head on, reorganizing the GMCC to set it on firm financial footing and transform it into an organization capable of promoting a business-oriented vision for Miami. Located in luxurious offices a block from the *Miami Herald* and near downtown Miami, the GMCC would become an influential force, rapidly growing from 750 members in 1984 to 3,500 members by the end of 1989 (and over 4,000 in 2000). It now includes dozens of specialized committees and subcommittees that carry out lobbying at the local, state, and federal levels.

Chapman, however, did not stop his drive for action and efficiency there. Composed of many small and medium-sized businesses and relatively few major corporations, organized around multiple committees and relatively open to outside scrutiny, by its very nature the GMCC can be a clumsy vehicle for wielding power. Chapman also secretly organized an informal group of the CEOs of the area's largest corporations under a telling name, the Non-Group.

Together, the GMCC and the Non-Group engineered a two-billion-dollar construction surge they baptized "the Decade of Progress." The effort produced a light rail system serving downtown. A campus of Miami-Dade Community College was built in close proximity to both the business district and to the city's oldest black neighborhood, once known as Colored Town or the Central Negro District, and now called Overtown. The college offered key educational opportunities, especially to the city's burgeoning immigrant population, and carried out myriad cultural activities and community events, which brought together an unusually diverse representation of Miami's racial and ethnic groups. Next to the college, a brand new public housing building for the elderly went up. Two blocks away, an upscale waterfront shopping and entertainment center, Bayside, built by the Rouse Corporation, was inaugurated. The Miami Arena, home of the expansion professional basketball team Miami Heat and the professional hockey team Florida Panthers, was built in an area inhabited by a large homeless population. Just over ten years later, another arena was built a few blocks away on the waterfront. In another area of downtown, a towering government center was built; across the street a new main library, a historical museum, and a fine arts center opened their doors. Next on the drawing board was a performing arts center. New buildings, however, did not produce social peace. Repeatedly, Miami's Cubans and black Americans challenged white Americans' vision of Miami.

MIAMI'S CUBAN TAKEOVER

"We Cuban people have made Miami. Thanks to the freedoms here in America, we're combining our natural Cuban energies with American knowledge, American know-how, to create a new, more passionate American. We immigrants, these new Americans, are going to be key players in reconstructing the new Cuba once Fidel leaves. We're going to make Cuba the next Japan!"

This Miami Cuban executive's assertion personifies the alternative view that so frustrates Miami's white American business leaders. Not only does this Miami Cuban give no credit to those who established the city and, more recently, constructed public colleges and universities, public transit, and arenas and revitalized much of the city, but his comments indicate a greater commitment to rebuilding Cuba than developing Miami.

For their first two decades in Miami, Miami's Cubans focused on reestablishing themselves economically and socially in the United States. They perceived no contradiction between making it in Miami and awaiting their presumed imminent return to Cuba. After all, they initiated the process of refurbishing Miami into the capital of the Caribbean, linking it to its colonial roots in the Spanish empire. They accordingly did not see a need to become Americans in the narrow U. S. sense.

Quite unintentionally, the federal and local public sectors provided tremendous indirect, seldom acknowledged aid to Miami Cubans, which greatly advanced their endeavors. Through the 1960s and 1970s, boosted by massive federal support for Cuban refugees, local government responded relatively quickly to the cubanization of Miami. In 1962, the Dade County School Board, which had no Latino members at the time, approved the first contemporary experiment in bilingual education. Federal funds made the choice relatively easy. It did not cost the school board anything, and the Miami Cuban community contained many trained professionals who could implement the bilingual program. Nevertheless, the bilingual program distinguished Miami from many cities and towns in the southwest United States that had bilingual education funds available and still resisted implementing such programs. In 1973, the County Commission, which also had no Latino representation at the time, declared Dade County officially bilingual and bicultural.

Federal aid, although a lesser amount per capita, had been provided to other immigrants, and at least some public sector institutions in other parts of the United States had advocated multiculturalism. Nowhere else, however, did it take off as in Miami. The public support undoubtedly helped, but equally important were the Miami Cubans themselves. The Miami Cubans contained a large segment of the professional and business class of pre-Castro Cuba. They were an integrated elite already. While Fidel had confiscated much of their property, they still had their experience and expertise. Government support permitted them to reestablish themselves quickly, to become the most vibrant, rapidly growing Latino business community in the United States and to propel Miami to become the capital of the Caribbean.

As they prospered and succeeded in Miami, Miami Cuban business leaders, however, did not join mainstream American business organizations. Rather than becoming part of the Greater Miami Chamber of Commerce, they participated in the Camara de Comercio Latino (COMACOL). Rather than petitioning for entry into the South Florida Builders' Association, they formed the Latin Builders' Association. Rather than contributing to the American Cancer Society, they supported La Liga Contra Cancer. Miami's Cubans were relatively satisfied with their regained status as they awaited Fidel's imminent fall, which was predicted daily on local Miami Cuban radio stations.

The Mariel boatlift of 1980, however, forced Miami Cubans to realize that while they may have created the capital of the Caribbean, they were still in the America of the United States, not Latin America. In 1980, over 125,000 Cubans migrated to South Florida, ferried by private boats chartered by Miami Cubans from the Cuban port of Mariel. Miami Cubans were hoping both to embarrass Fidel by aiding their compatriots' flight from his dictatorship and to reunite with relatives who had remained in Cuba. Some did find their relatives, but many others came in an uncontrollable flood. Newly arrived Cuban refugees camped temporarily under freeways and in public parks. Moreover, Fidel determined who left Cuba. It was not just the relatives of Miami Cubans. The boats took whomever the Cubans put on them, and that included released prisoners and mental patients along with "regular" Cubans. South Florida's Americans, along with the rest of the United States, focused not on the flight to freedom, but on the disruption and chaos it caused. Rather than embarrassing Fidel, the Mariel boatlift produced a massive backlash against Cuban refugees. The *Miami Herald* strongly editorialized against the boatlift, along with virtually every national media outlet. Miami's Cubans realized they were not as integrated or accepted as they had thought.

Rather than admitting defeat or minimizing their visible presence, they responded forcefully and in typical American fashion. They formed ethnic organizations, engaged in ethnic lobbying, and became involved in local and national politics. The federal and local support of the Miami Cuban community may have helped them gain strength, but what powered their ethnic organizing most potently was the prejudice they suddenly encountered from the broader society. In the 1980s, Miami Cubans emerged as a visible force that could no longer be ignored.

Two parallel elites had emerged in Miami. The Miami Cuban elite had previously assumed a low profile and been accordingly relatively ignored by the white American local elite. But from the 1980s onward, white American leaders could no longer ignore Miami's Cubans. A 1988 study of top leadership conducted by *The Miami Herald* revealed the transformation. Of 18 individuals identified as top leaders, 10 were American whites (56 percent). The other 8 (44 percent) were all Miami Cubans. That was more than the Cuban share of the population of the metropolitan area. A 2000 *Herald* survey of 406 government positions, indicated that white Americans still have disproportionate power as they held 51 percent of elected and top appointed jobs, compared to 32 percent for Latinos (all but 5 percent of whom are Cuban American; Branch-Brioso 2000a).

Not only did individual Cubans rise to positions of power, but the Miami Cuban community also challenged and defeated the white American agenda. In 1986 Miami's white American leadership proposed to add one cent to the local sales tax in order to finance the construction of a performing arts center. Miami's Cuban small businesses revolted. They saw no need for an extra penny from their customers to service white American elite needs. Miami Cuban radio stations rallied against the initiative and for the first time in the white American elite's memory, one of their initiatives failed. A newspaper executive recounted: "The traditional leadership in Dade County had an ultimate comeuppance as far as Latinos are concerned the day that penny sales tax was clobbered due to the leadership of the Latino Community—that was a watershed experience for the leadership of our community."

WHITE AMERICANS' AMBIVALENT CONCESSIONS

The 1986 defeat of the penny sales tax resolved the white American elite to abandon the policy of waiting for Miami's Cubans to come to their side. The American white leadership could no longer afford the luxury of shutting out Latinos. Besides needing support for political initiatives, Latino customers were important to many businesses, as were Latino executives, managers, and employees. Organizations such as United

Way relied on contributions from Latino workers and cooperation from Latino managers and owners to meet their fundraising goals. If American whites continued to ignore Miami's Cubans, they could no longer advance their own agenda. White "Americans" actively began to incorporate Latinos in elite circles, especially Latino executives from large American banks, corporations, and law firms. They elected Latinos to the chairmanship of key civic organizations, such as the United Way of Dade County and the GMCC. Latino membership in the chamber increased from about 5 percent at the beginning of the 1980s to over a third at the end of the decade. A white American banker with close ties with the chamber stated:

> Well, the chamber is a very interesting study all by itself. In the mid-1980s, there were eight hundred members and it was 90 percent Anglos and 9 percent Hispanic and 1 percent black. Five years later, it was probably 55 percent Anglo and the balance largely Hispanic and it had grown from eight hundred to four thousand members. In 1989, we got a Hispanic leader. The Executive Committee of the chamber's representation is not just token—we have blacks, women, Hispanics for the first time. We try to identify leadership, bring that leadership along to be interested in the whole community. The chamber today is amongst the strongest leadership institutions in this community.

While elite organizations attempted to recruit blacks during this time—and did to a certain extent—the pace and depth of Latino incorporation was much greater. There are many more Latinos than blacks in the Greater Miami Chamber of Commerce, and at higher levels. This is not surprising given that there were many more Latino business owners and professionals, both relatively and absolutely, than blacks in similar roles. More interestingly, perhaps, is the fact that within elite organizations, committees that dealt with primarily black problems were attended mostly by blacks and some American whites. Those that dealt with Latinos were attended by Latinos and a scattering of American whites. There was virtually no black-Latino crossover.

White American leaders were proud of their inclusiveness. They felt that the leading civic organizations in Miami were now open to Latinos with the right talents and attitudes. A white American executive argued:

> One group ought to be singled out and that is the United Way. I really feel it represents the ultimate, positive dynamics of what a community ought to be. You have on that board all the groups, all parts of the community. Everyone is adjusted. We don't sit around and talk about problems without understanding each other. They are not tokens that are brought on. They have to earn their way on the board. It all represents the diversity of the community. You are on the leading edge of getting things done, especially in the inner city. I am talking about the leadership in the intercultural relationship. The dynamics of that board, sixty people, is fascinating to me.

Since white Americans were extending themselves to incorporate Miami Cubans, the continuation of parallel Miami Cuban business and service institutions frequently frustrated American white elites. They expected assimilation into *their* organizations, while the alternative Latino business organizations should fade away. They desired a unified business community with the American whites in the lead and Miami Cubans having become Americans, speaking English and adopting what they viewed as American civic values.

> There is no impediment for any Hispanic to be involved in anything they desire in Miami. There are no barriers. With intelligence and money, anything can be achieved. But thousands don't want to get involved further than their activities in the Latin Chamber of Commerce. I just found out that Miami ranks thirty-seventh out of fifty in United Way contributions, and this is because a majority of citizens, Hispanics, don't care to give. All this is so sad, disappointing and a good barometer of how things are. United Way is a leveler, but even when headed by a Cuban one year, it didn't make any difference.

The businessman's explanation for the problem is cultural, but that insight hardly tempers his pique:

> I think there is a problem there and I think it has to do with the way people have been brought up. They are very generous in their home, very generous in their socializing, and they spend money, but when it comes to real down-to-earth charity, they are not as charitable as they should be. People who are earning their livelihood here, and especially people who came destitute, with nothing, and made a very good life for themselves, should pay back somehow. I would say that I get frustrated with their lack of participation in the things they should.

A white American banker offered a somewhat different interpretation of the problem:

> As non-Hispanics understand the cultural differences around them, I think Hispanics have to do the same. And that includes the understanding of the concept of volunteerism, an American tradition, and this is more critical here because of cutbacks and enormous needs. It's a problem for the concept to be readily adopted by so many who come from countries where the government handles everything. Fifty percent of the people who benefit from the work of United Way are Hispanics, and yet Hispanics have the sense that this is an Anglo-only organization.

Many American whites harbored similarly strong resentment about what they perceived as another example of the lack of acculturation to U. S. values among Miami Cubans. They continued to focus on Cuba and the intense anticommunism of local Spanish-language radio stations. A prominent American white lawyer complained:

> Hispanic radio is one of the worst culprits. It foments revolution. I would go to the FCC to have them censored, but I admit there might be no basis for this. I'm a first-amendment person, and although I don't agree with them in their urging Hispanics to vote Hispanic despite the candidate's capabilities, I am tolerant of their

right to say this. But the labeling of people as communists! I would sue the son of a bitch! I wouldn't put up with that for a minute. You can say vote for someone because he's Cuban even though he is less qualified, but this is different than calling someone a communist.

Although the American white leadership felt that "bringing the Latinos to the table" was progress, some Latinos, and especially many Miami Cubans, increasingly felt a sense of ownership that contrasted sharply with the white American notion of them as outsiders being allowed into the game. With a growing power base of their own and substantial economic resources, many Latino leaders could afford to decline what they perceived as condescending or patronizing invitations. A Miami media executive described the process: "The (American white) civic leadership invited *some* Latins to come to *their* place, sit at *their* table, and play by *their* rules."

THE 'MIAMI HERALD' AS VOICE OF THE WHITE AMERICANS

The *Miami Herald*, once the flagship newspaper of the Knight Ridder chain, epitomizes the ambivalence and difficulties white American leaders have had with the alternative Latino elite and community. As in other cities, the primary newspaper is viewed by many as the voice of the collective power structure (Molotch 1976). It strives to give an objective, or at least balanced, approach to community issues. Frequently, it also endeavors to find and express a unified, consensus view of what the community is and should be. The *Miami Herald* took this task seriously. The Knight brothers, who purchased the *Miami Herald* in 1939, consistently argued that newspapers had a responsibility not only for journalistic excellence, but also for service to the common welfare of the community they serve. As already indicated, Knight Ridder Chairman Alvah Chapman took the lead in the 1970s and 1980s in forging consensus, at least for the white American leaders.

The emerging Latino community, however, presented special challenges to the *Herald*, both in terms of building consensus and in maintaining the importance of the *Herald* as a voice of the community power structure. While the population of Miami had grown consistently ever since Cubans started arriving in the 1960s, subscription rates to the *Miami Herald* had lagged. Knight Ridder's annual reports implied that the *Miami Herald* was still doing well, but those on the inside reported that advertising revenues and profits were declining. Drastic new measures were warranted.

The *Miami Herald* had been publishing an international edition for Latin America and the Caribbean since 1946, but it had not done much to specifically address the growing Latino population in Miami. As with all other major newspapers in the United States, the primary audience was English speakers. It was expected that immigrants would assimilate enough to read English. The newspaper might write articles about immigrant communities, but they would be in English and most likely written by American reporters, at least bilingual Americanized reporters. Foreign-language newspapers were left to the ethnic community, as in the case of the *Diario las Americas*, which is owned by Nicaraguans and has been publishing a Spanish-language daily in Miami since the 1960s. Mainstream American journalism was decidedly English only.

In 1977, however, the *Miami Herald* took an unprecedented, decisive step when it began publication of a daily Spanish-language edition, *El Herald*. *El Herald* marked the first time a U. S. newspaper chain had published a Spanish-language edition. With this, a key actor within the local business elite acknowledged the need to speak to the Other in his or her own language, albeit perhaps only grudgingly and for a very compelling business need rather than out of cultural enlightenment.

Nevertheless, its Spanglish name (correct Spanish would be *El Heraldo*) attests to the ambivalence with which *Herald* executives viewed the effort. *Herald* management envisioned *El Herald* as a transitional product, an American newspaper in Spanish that would last only as long as assimilation had not been completed. Indeed, most of its content was a straight translation of articles that appeared in the English edition. *El Herald* had no independence and few resources, but it symbolically represented a momentous transformation for the American management of the *Miami Herald.*

Pragmatically, however, the production of a weak correlative did not impress Miami's Cubans. It was in their language, but it was not of their community. They pointed out that not only were most articles simply translations of the English edition, but the few Latino reporters they had were more likely to be Puerto Rican or Mexican. The content and especially the editorial positions were not consonant with Miami Cubans' primary anti-Castro and more general anticommunist passions. In 1987, the Cuban-American National Foundation purchased a full-page advertisement in the *Herald* that asserted, "The *Miami Herald* is aggressive in its ignorance of our people. It refuses to understand that Cuban Americans see the struggle between totalitarianism and democracy as a personal, ever-present struggle, We live the struggle daily because our friends and families enslaved in communist Cuba live it daily (Cuban American National Foundation 1987).

The Cuban American National Foundation and its creator, Jorge Mas Canosa, had emerged in the early 1980s as the most vocal and persistent voice of Miami's Cuban community. It was a voice that belied white American assumptions regarding the Americanization and assimilation of Cubans. CANF fixated on Fidel's Cuba, and Mas Canosa, until his death in the mid-1990s, seemed to focus on becoming president of post-Castro Cuba. With an assist from the Reagan administration and the support of dozens of well-heeled Cuban Americans, who contributed a minimum of $10,000 annually for a seat on the board or $5,000 to serve as trustees, CANF was remarkably successful in influencing U. S. policy toward Cuba (Kiger 1997).

The *Herald* also sought to serve other local foreign-language communities, periodically publishing sections of the paper in Haitian Creole and Portuguese (for Brazilians), but the Spanish-language edition received the most resources and generated the greatest backlash. Given the orientation of Miami's Cubans, the half-hearted effort embodied in *El Herald* failed either to lift subscription rates or to bring Miami's Latinos into the mainstream American organizations. However, perhaps because of the need for profits and the rhetorical fury of Jorge Mas Canosa and CANF, the *Herald* and Knight Ridder intensified their efforts rather than giving up. In 1987, it created a brand-new Spanish-language newspaper, *El Nuevo Herald*, which was virtually independent of the English edition. It had its own building, its own reporting staff, and most importantly, its own editors, overwhelmingly Cuban Americans.

Not surprisingly, the editorial stance of *El Nuevo Herald* became more decidedly Miami Cuban and anti-Castro, and less mainstream American. By the end of the 1980s, the newspaper reflected the conservative discourse of the exile community more than the often liberal outlook of its English sister publication. Not only was it editorializing in favor of admitting Latin American immigrants into the country but, far more than any other U. S. daily, it covered events in Cuba. It referred to Castro as a dictator, not as the president of Cuba, and it had constant anti-Castro opinion pieces. It even gave a job on its editorial page to a man who had once chained himself to the *Herald*'s building to protest the paper's Cuba coverage. The *Miami Herald*, and specifically *El Nuevo Herald*, acknowledged the need for the Other not merely to be spoken to in his own language, but also to speak in his or her own voice.

Even the English-language *Miami Herald*'s 1989 decision to hire David Lawrence as publisher, a staunch devotee of the Knight brothers' civic journalism, was partly motivated by its desire to placate the Miami Cuban community (Lizza 2000). When Lawrence arrived in Miami, he took lessons in Spanish and was tutored in the cultural nuances of the Latino community by a Cuban American professor. In a Sunday opinion piece, he then called on everyone to follow his example. He hailed multicultural Miami as an example to the entire nation and as being at the "cutting edge" of the America to come. He urged fellow Miamians to "get on" and enroll in a foreign language class (Lawrence 1991).

Nonetheless, some ambivalence remained at Knight Ridder. It was first inscribed in the very name of the newspaper, two-thirds in Spanish *(El Nuevo)*, one-third in English *(Herald)*. More importantly, Miami Cubans continued to attack the *Herald* as too liberal. The newspaper still occasionally expressed opinions different from Miami's implacable anti-Castro anti-communists. In 1992, the *Miami Herald* editorialized against the Torricelli Bill, which tightened U. S. sanctions against Cuba, and a Cuban columnist for *El Nuevo Herald* wrote an editorial highly critical of exile leader Jorge Mas Canosa. CANF chairman, Jorge Mas Canosa, who had championed the legislation, was furious. Mas Canosa went on the airwaves to launch a campaign against the paper. He blasted the paper as a tool of Castro's regime and called for a boycott. *Herald* vending machines were smeared with feces. Staffers received death threats. Advertisers were targeted with letter-writing campaigns. Publisher David Lawrence began starting his car in the morning with a remote-control device, and city buses carried huge ads reading "Yo no creo en el *Herald*"(I don't believe in the *Herald*).

In 1998, it appeared as if Knight Ridder's leaders had given up on Miami. The CEO of Knight Ridder announced that corporate headquarters would be moved to California's Silicon Valley, home of Knight Ridder's *San Jose Mercury News.* Knight Ridder corporate spokespersons claimed the move would position them better for the changes in journalism tied to the Internet. Alvah Chapman, retired and honorary chair of Knight Ridder, lamented the move, however. A few months later, the publisher of the *Miami Herald,* David Lawrence, announced his retirement. As its new publisher, the *Herald* hired Alberto Ibarguen, the half-Cuban publisher of *El Nuevo Herald* and a friend of Mas Canosa (who had died in 1997). *El Nuevo Herald* had achieved the highest circulation of any Spanish-language daily in the United States. More significantly, it had been transformed from a pale reflection of white American interests to a consistent voice of Miami Cubans.

Through the 1980s and 1990s, Miami's white American leaders actively reached out to incorporate Miami's Cubans into white American institutions. They met with limited success. Many Cubans and other

Latino businesspeople did join the chamber of commerce and assume leadership positions in various organizations. They did not, however, abandon their Cuban culture, a refusal that frustrated white Americans. The 1999–2000 Elián Gonzalez affair revealed how deep divisions still remained.

THE TRIALS OF ELIÁN

As recounted in chapter one, Elián divided Miami, with Latinos, primarily Cubans, advocating that he remain in Miami and non-Latinos (along with a few Latinos) arguing that he should be reunited with his father in Cuba. Passions permeated interpersonal relations, even with total strangers. María Hernández, a Colombian married to a Miami Cuban, was driving to work when a pickup flying American flags pulled up beside her at a stoplight. The pickup driver, thinking she was a Cuban, rolled down a window and made an obscene gesture (Bragg 2000a).

The pickup driver's gesture may have been extreme, but his opinion was typical. Polls showed both white and black Americans felt strongly that the boy belonged with his father. Indeed, the pollster who conducted the study, Rob Schroth, claimed, "In twenty years of studying polls in Dade, I have never seen results that set Cubans and the other two groups so far apart on an issue. The contrast is the starkest I've ever seen. It is truly a tale of two cities." About 90 percent of blacks and 80 percent of whites disapproved of County Mayor Penelas's threats to deny federal agents the help of county police in repatriating Elián and of his attempt to blame any resulting violence on Reno and President Clinton. At least three-fourths of Cuban Americans, however, approved of both statements and of Penelas's overall performance (Viglucci and Marrero 2000). Garth Reeves, the former publisher of Miami's black newspaper, the *Miami Times*, claimed, "The Cuban exiles have shown such arrogance. They're saying, 'This is our town now, and, damn it, we run it. We make the decisions,' to the exclusion of everyone else."

Reeves asserted that Cuban Americans "are a pampered minority that became a pampered majority, and now—at the first major setback for them in recent history—they denigrate the country that gave them a haven" (Bragg 2000a).

These reactions from non-Latinos were not, however, simply primordial anti-immigrant feelings that had only been waiting for the right moment to emerge. While some, perhaps even many, non-Latinos do harbor anti-Cuban sentiments, the Elián affair revealed that the form, expression, and perhaps even the existence of these feelings emerged out of interactions between Miami Cubans and non-Cubans. For years, Ann-Sofi Truby and a Miami Cuban who does maintenance at her house in South Miami had talked "about our families, different things," according to Ms. Truby, who has lived in Miami for nearly thirty years. They stopped talking, however, during the Elián situation. "I would stay inside while he was here," she said, because talk would end in argument. Ms. Truby, who is in her sixties, was one of the thousands who bought an American flag. She waved it from her Volvo whenever she saw people demonstrating to keep Elián in the United States (Bragg 2000a). Similarly, many younger Miami Cubans who had never before seriously considered their ethnic identity, who had believed that they were Americans because they were different from their parents and grandparents, suddenly discovered that they too could feel Cuban when the "real Americans" condemned them.

Heightened ethnic attachments were ubiquitous, but high-profile Cuban American celebrities and politicians advanced them considerably. Cuban American celebrities Gloria Estefan and Andy García expressed their support for Elián. Local Cuban politicians were, nevertheless, the most forceful. While Elián was still at his relatives' house in Miami, County Mayor Penelas defiantly warned President Clinton and Attorney General Janet Reno that they would be held responsible if any blood was shed when taking Elián from his Miami family's home. Both Penelas and City of Miami Mayor Carollo claimed their local police departments would not assist federal agents if they came to Miami to remove Elián, although Penelas subsequently clarified that police would keep the peace. City Police Chief William O'Brien did not forewarn Mayor Carollo before the raid. After the raid, an angry Carollo publicly stated that the police chief should be fired. The mayor's hand-picked city manager, Donald Warshaw—the only one with authority to fire the chief—refused. Carollo then fired the city manager and the following day the police chief resigned. Cuban Americans replaced both.

The Cuban American National Foundation jumped on the issue. Within hours of the boy's rescue from Florida waters, CANF converted Elián literally into a poster child, distributing thousands of leaflets of him at the World Trade Organization meeting in Seattle, beneath the headline,: "Another child victim of Fidel Castro." After polls indicated that both young and old Cubans and other Latinos in Miami overwhelmingly believed that Elián should remain with his Miami relatives rather than return to Cuba to live with his father, CANF aggressively sought to incorporate younger Miami Cubans into an organization that had primarily appealed to older exiles. It appointed a new, younger executive director, a thirty-five-year-old American-born Cuban, Joe García. García became the first CANF executive director born outside of Cuba. He promised a reinvigorated foundation, with more sophisticated media efforts to educate the American people about Cuba (de Valle 2000). They also appointed a non-Cuban former State Department expert on Cuba to head its Washington office and committed to an expansion that included purchasing a new building on Capitol Hill, refurbishing a historic landmark in Miami where Cuban refugees were processed in the 1960s, and doubling both their staff and annual budget. Not neglecting their traditional political role, CANF also singled out districts of Congressional adversaries for television advertisements, pledging to spend "whatever it takes" to protect the unyielding American policy it helped to create (Marquis 2000).

All of these efforts undoubtedly increased solidarity among Miami Cubans, even Cubans in the rest of the United States. Twenty-nine-year-old Cristina Portuondo, for example, grew up in a small Virginia town, spoke with a Southern twang, and had little visible connection to Miami's exile community. But after Elián had been reunited with his father and taken to Washington, D.C., she ended up demonstrating in front of the Washington home of Cuba's top diplomat in the United States. "Here I am, a Cuban from Virginia and I'm one of the main ones that's been organizing," said Portuondo, who writes computer manuals for a living. "I've declared myself" (Robles 2000).

The *Miami Herald*, which seeks to maintain journalistic objectivity, also found itself riven by the Elián affair. Liz Balmaseda, a Pulitzer Prize-winning columnist complained to both the *Herald*'s publisher and its editor about what she saw as the paper's unsympathetic coverage of Miami's Cuban community. Fabiola Santiago, a senior writer at the *Herald*, felt the paper did a poor job of explaining how Cuban children were oppressed under Castro's regime (McQueen 2000). When Meg Laughlin wrote a detailed account of Elián's private school and the right-wing textbooks used there, she came under fire from Barbara Gutierrez, the reader representative for the *Herald*, who leads a weekly critique of the paper's coverage. "The tone sounded editorial," Gutierrez says. "I think the message got through. There are certain ways of reporting a story where a community might feel it's inflammatory." A front-page editorial ordered by publisher Alberto Ibarguen declared: "The scenes of overwhelming force from yesterday at dawn shock the conscience. . . . The evidence clearly suggests that the Miami relatives were at last prepared to voluntarily deliver Elián to his father within a very short time." The *Herald*'s reporting, however, would undermine this contention in the following days.

Yet, closer examination reveals the difficulty, perhaps even impossibility, of attaining "objectivity" on such an emotional issue. As the Herald's Gutierrez points out, "In this highly emotional story, what sounds straightforward to one group of readers sounds like pandering to another. . . . Each side wants the newspaper to report the news from their perspective." Position and passion is even inscribed in simple descriptive vocabulary. Roberto Vizcon, the news director of a Spanish-language television station, indicated, "We would never broadcast that the boy is threatened with going back home. We would say, the boy is threatened with going back to Cuba. . . . And we would never call Fidel Castro president." To these Miami Cubans, Castro must be referred to as a dictator (McQueen 2000).

Regardless of whether the *Miami Herald* and other local media outlets were objective or not, the Elián affair generated a tremendous backlash from white and black Americans. City hall was pelted with bananas, picking up on a local university professor's reference a couple of years before to Miami's "banana-republic" government. County Mayor Penelas received numerous email messages that blasted his statements that he would not assist federal officials in their efforts to reunite Elián with his father. "My husband and I have been residents of Dade County for over forty years and we have never been as angry or embarrassed at a speech by a Dade County mayor as the absurd speech you made yesterday. You are mayor of Cuban and Latins only, and the other residents of Dade County have no mayor. I can assure you that if there is a recall movement for you, we will sign it immediately. We will also do whatever we can to ensure you are not elected to office again. We are totally appalled, angry, and humiliated by this situation." Arthur Teele Jr., the City of Miami's only black commissioner, claimed, "A number of people here are concerned and outraged because they believe the city of Miami has lost its balance and equilibrium." He added that Mayor Carollo's city government seemed anxious to exclude all but Cuban Americans precisely when interethnic tensions were running high (Bragg 2000b).

David Abraham, a professor at the University of Miami, explained, "This became a bizarre experience where family, flag, and police—all parts of the Republican trinity—were attacked by Cuban Americans. There was the firing of the police chief because he kept public order, and the desecration of the flag, and it was very disconcerting to middle Americans" (Bragg 2000b).

The Elián affair had similar negative national repercussions for Miami's Cuban community. Suddenly, the rest of America, who had previously cared little about Cuba, was paying attention to Cuba and Miami's Cubans. Jim McDermott, Democratic representative from Washington, maintained that Miami's Cubans "showed what they were really all about. They were ready to sacrifice one of their own kids, and they didn't really care about separating him from his father." For the first time since Fidel Castro assumed power forty years earlier, the U. S. Congress seriously considered easing the embargo on Cuba.

Both Cuban American and non-Cuban American leaders in Miami expressed concern that the Elián issue was tearing apart the community and giving Miami a bad image. White American county manager Merritt Steirheim claimed, "Nobody in this town was without trauma: Cuban American, Haitian, Anglo, African American—everybody had anger, remorse, pain. My hope is that it was cathartic. The residue from Elián will be important for many, many years. We have a lot of wounds to heal."

Miami-Dade County's Community Relations Board (CRB), a residual of the civil rights era whose mission is to promote harmony among ethnic groups, proved ineffectual, as it was as riven by division as the broader community. During the relative ethnic calm of the 1990s, the county reduced funding and attention to the CRB to the extent that it did not even have a full-time director. When the Elián affair struck, the agency was totally unprepared. In the wake of its failure, Mayor Penelas urged a reorganization and the county manager requested $300,000 for six new CRB positions, including a full-time director (Branch-Brioso 2000a).

A few prominent Miami Cuban leaders even began to condemn their fellow Miami Cubans, claiming that their focus on Elián and Castro's Cuba was myopic, that it was hurting the Miami community. Some Miami Cuban leaders sought to ease tensions at the same time as they wanted to be able to explain to non-Cubans why they felt so strongly that Elián should remain in the United States even if his father wanted to return with him to Cuba. Reflecting the convergence of Latino and white American business elites, representatives from Mesa Redonda, an organization of Latino business and civic leaders, privately met with the city of Miami's mayor, Joe Carollo, and asked him to tone down his rhetoric, to try to build bridges to the rest of the community. Mesa Redonda then had a joint meeting with the "Non-Group," the most important non-Hispanic white organization, and Broulé, a black leadership fraternity. They jointly resolved to work toward unifying the community. Miami Cubans and non-Cubans alike seemingly agreed on only one point—over 80 percent of each of these populations agreed that the events surrounding the Elián González affair hurt the interests of the Cuban-American community (Viglucci and Marrero 2000).

The federal raid to extricate Elián Gonzalez from the Little Havana home of his great uncle Lázaro Gonzalez unleashed enormous passions in the Cuban American community. The theme of betrayal by the American government, especially by "liberals" and "Democrats," has resonated in the Cuban American mind ever since the Bay of Pigs. The raid was seen as the second great betrayal, and it unleashed a spate of violence in Little Havana, followed some days later by a peaceful mass protest. For many Miami Cubans, particularly the hard-liners in the community, the 2000 election became a way to channel the anger and impotence they felt about the Clinton administration's handling of the Elián affair and their more general frustration about what they considered the administration's accommodating policy toward the Castro regime.

Despite candidate Al Gore's efforts to distance himself from the Clinton administration on the issue, the resentment among anti-Castro groups in the Miami Cuban community soon rebounded in the form of votes. In the 1990s, Democrats had made some inroads among Miami's Cubans. The Republicans were in an anti-immigration mood in the mid-1990s, and some of their policies directly threatened the welfare of elderly Cuban Americans who were not citizens. In addition, in the 1992 campaign Bill Clinton took a position to the right of President George Bush by supporting the Torricelli, or "Cuban Democracy," Act. Thus, while in the 1980s Democrats obtained an average of 17 percent of the Cuban American vote in national elections, that figure rose to 34 percent in the 1990s (Branch-Brioso 2000b).

In the 2000 election, the Democratic share of the Cuban American vote dropped to 18 percent. Most analysts believe that the Elián controversy played a major role in this swing (along with Jeb Bush's popularity among Cuban Americans and Republican moderation on immigration), which, representing several thousand votes, was more than enough to determine the Florida, and thus the national, election.

Some Miami Cubans saw the outcome as a sign of divine retribution. Had Elián not been saved by a miracle? Now those who had ignored that he was a blessed child destined to live in freedom were being punished. In a sense, the oddball 2000 election did represent a miracle of sorts. Miami's Cuban hard-liners lost big in the Elián case, taking a huge hit in public opinion. Even Republicans in Congress had begun lobbying against the embargo, as had the farm lobby and the U. S. Chamber of Commerce. Cuban-Americans, with a population equivalent to 0.4 percent of the U. S. total, had accomplished much by first promoting and later maintaining a hard-line U. S. policy toward Cuba, but now all those accomplishments were in danger. The 2000 election was the answer to the prayers of the Cuban-American hard-liners.

How could Cuban-American hard-liners persuade a Republican administration that their dollars and votes were as crucial as those of the farm states and the agriculture and business lobbies? It might happen if Florida decided the presidential election, the state was decided by a few hundred or thousand votes, and the Cuban American vote swung significantly from one candidate or party for ideological reasons. And that's what happened. The election gave Miami's Cuban conservatives in Florida a sense of victory, revenge, and entitlement. They immediately began to lobby for a tougher U. S. policy toward Cuba, and were favored by the new administration with some key appointments

Even after the election, Elián continued to exercise his influence over interethnic relations and politics in Miami. At the end of 2000, the University of Miami, a private university that receives some funding from

the State of Florida for its medical school, announced that it would hire
as its next president Donna Shalala, President Clinton's Secretary of
Health and Human Services. Two Cuban American state legislators,
Mario Diaz-Balart and Carlos Lacasa, objected. Diaz-Balart claimed
Shalala's appointment was offensive "to Miami's Hispanic community
because she is part of the administration that put a gun to a six-year-old's
head." Lacasa, chair of the state's House Budget Committee, indicated
that he was ready to evaluate the University of Miami's claim on the dollars (Driscoll 2000). Immediately, the *Miami Herald* received numerous
letters to the editor, many from Miami Cubans, condemning Diaz-
Balart and Lacasa ("Holding UM Hostage" 2000). The *Herald* published
their own editorial criticizing the state legislator's comments ("Misplaced Politics" 2000), and Carlos de la Cruz Sr., the Cuban American
chair of the University of Miami Board of Trustees, defended the appointment (Steinback 2001). The legislators soon backed off.

More striking and surprising has been the shift in policy of the Cuban
American National Foundation. Through the 1980s and 1990s, CANF,
the best-funded Cuban American lobbying organization, led the anti-
Castro forces in Washington and locally. They fought successfully for
tightening the embargo on Cuba and helped establish Radio and TV
Martí, which aim their broadcasts at Cuba. They viewed the Elián case
as a mechanism to reinvigorate the organization with younger members. After Attorney General Janet Reno declared that Elián belonged
with his father, Alberto Hernandez, a director of CANF, urged other
exiled leaders to take action immediately, with the objective of paralyzing Miami and the airport. From the beginning of the Elián affair, Jorge
Mas Santos, CANF chairman and son of CANF founder Jorge Mas
Canosa, was a fixture at every press conference held by the Miami relatives or their attorneys. When Elián visited his Cuban-born grandmoth-
ers at the Miami Beach home of Sister Jeanne O'Laughlin, Mas Santos
drove the child to the meeting. After dropping off the child, Mas Santos
went to a neighbor's home, where he tried to spy on the meeting. More
recently, Elián's cousins and other family members had flown to Wash-

ington aboard Mas Santos's jet to meet with members of Congress in an effort to arrange for the boy's citizenship (DeFede 2000).

The effort led to an unanticipated policy change. In April 2001, Miami announced that it would host the second Latin Grammys ceremony (Levin 2001). The previous year, CANF led the political opposition to Miami hosting the event because they recognized and even gave awards to groups from Cuba and to individuals who had not renounced Castro (Steinback 2001). CANF's position, also held by other anti-Castroites, was supported by a Miami-Dade County ordinance that prohibited the county from doing business with anyone who had ties to Cuba. In 1999, following complaints by Miami officials, the City of Miami cancelled a concert by the Cuban band Los Van Van to be held in a city-owned auditorium. Los Van Van subsequently played at another arena, while thousands protested.

In 2001, CANF, along with local media stars Gloria and Emilio Estefan and the tourism industry, led the fight to obtain the Grammys ceremony for Miami ("A Latin Music Prize" 2001). CANF President Mas Santos even defended the Grammys on the vicious airwaves of Miami Cuban talk radio. The first time, he got nowhere and vowed never to go back (Balmaseda 2001b). After a few months of diligent radio work by Mas Santos, the same microphones suddenly began to sing the praises of "Los Grammys." Mas Santos spoke about an exile population that defended "tolerance, freedom of expression, and democracy." American whites who had previously expressed frustration at the intransigent Cubans also became more tolerant. A spokesperson for the Grammys announced the academy's "heartfelt recognition of the pain and struggle of the people who call Cuba their nation"(Balmaseda 2001a).

Not all Miami Cuban opposition to the Grammys had been erased. While CANF and Miami-Dade County Mayor Penelas praised the Grammys, the Cuban exile group Presidio Politico Cubano, representing thirty-nine exile organizations, held a press conference to announce that it would not support the Latin Grammys if Cuban artists were included. At the same event, City of Miami Mayor Joe Carollo, who had earlier signed a letter supporting the Grammys in Miami, spoke in support of Presidio Politico and against Miami hosting the Grammys (Levin 2001). Similarly, in April 2001, Miami city officials tried to persuade the promoter of an international soccer tournament to move the event out of Miami, as there was a chance that the Cuban national soccer club would participate. "It's a matter of public safety," asserted Miami commissioner Tomas Regalado. "We don't need another Elián. The problem is if they come here and win and say, 'We dedicate this to our leader, Fidel Castro,' then what happens?" City of Miami mayor Joe Carollo declared, "I do not see Cuba playing at the Orange Bowl at all until you have a democracy in Cuba" (Kauffman 2001). Meanwhile, the Miami organization of Bay of Pigs veterans who had tried to invade and overthrow Castro's regime thirty years earlier remained intransigent. They banned two of their members who had traveled to Cuba and attended a conference on the Bay of Pigs invasion (Yanez 2001). In short, hard-line anti-Castroites persisted in Miami forty years after Castro assumed power in Cuba, but by then they had begun to lose power to a new generation of Miami Cubans, many of whom cared as much about Miami as they did about Cuba and Castro.

By the year 2000, Miami's Cubans had not quite taken over Miami, but they certainly had caused great consternation among the American white elite and forced them to change their ways. American whites still held two of every three positions of power in the county (Branch-Brioso, Henderson, and Chardy 2000), but Miami's Cubans dominated local elected offices, had wrested tremendous concessions from the largest local newspaper, and had forcefully demonstrated that Cuban politics are as much local and Miami-based as they are Washington-based. Both Miami Cubans and white Americans had changed, at least somewhat. Miami Cuban leaders still led the fight against Fidel Castro, but now they were both also concerned about interethnic relations in the broader community, and many of the most visible and powerful were willing to compromise. On the other hand, white Americans were seemingly changing themselves more than were the immigrant Cubans, although the dominant language of public issues remained English, even if often heavily accented, and many Cubans had joined mainstream American institutions.

BLACK FRUSTRATION: RIOTS AND BUSINESS DEVELOPMENT

The chairman of the New World Center Action Committee of the Greater Miami Chamber of Commerce (GMCC) called the meeting to order promptly at 8:00 a.m. Arranged around the table were representatives of many of Miami's most important businesses. The committee, one of the most influential within greater Miami's most powerful formal business organization, focuses on revitalizing the city's moribund downtown, the very project that Chapman, GMCC, and the Non-Group emphasized.

The day's agenda of the New World Center Action Committee did not include one item that was probably on the minds of many of the executives gathered that morning in the late 1980s at the GMCC office at the Omni, a hotel and shopping center complex on the periphery of the downtown district. A few days before, a Colombian-born City of Miami police officer had shot and killed a young black man on a motorcycle, whom the police officer claimed had tried to run him down. That event, which took place within easy walking distance of the site of the chamber meeting, was followed by rioting in sections of Overtown.

As always, the business at hand was conducted swiftly so that members could get to their jobs promptly. By the time of the committee meeting, things had calmed down, but some committee members still had the riot on their minds. The committee chairman, however, was apparently not one of them. Within forty-five minutes, the agenda had been concluded, and the chairman came to the standard request: "Any new business?"

"I think we should talk about the riot and what we can do about it," suggested one of the members, a woman. The chairman appeared surprised at the suggestion. He fumbled a bit before declaring, "I don't think that's really under the purview of this committee. There isn't much we can do about it." Another committee member agreed. "No, I think that falls under another committee. They should deal with it. What could we do anyway?" The meeting was adjourned.

In 1980, a major race riot convulsed Miami at the same time as 150,000 new immigrants from Cuba and Haiti flooded the area (Porter and Dunn 1984; Portes and Stepick 1993). By the time a curfew covering fifty-two square miles was lifted, the toll from the three days of rioting that began on May 17, 1980, stood at 18 dead, 3,000 jobs lost, 283 businesses burned and looted, and estimated damage of about $100 million (Whitefield 2000a).

Police brutality and the criminal justice system provoked the 1980 disturbance, as they have incited virtually all modern race riots in the United States (Lieberson and Silverman 1965). Police responded by focusing on social control. They obtained a dramatic increase in their budget, hired many more officers, and developed strategies to contain riots and limit loss of life and property damage. Verdicts in racially charged cases would no longer be announced late in the day or on weekends. Once the jury had reached a verdict in such a case, it would not be announced for several hours to allow the police to prepare for trouble. If a disturbance occurred, the area would be sealed off by police to prevent the kinds of attacks on motorists that had taken several lives in 1980, as well as to prevent outsiders from coming in to take advantage of the chaos. Meanwhile, rather than allowing rioters to take control of the streets, police would move in en masse to prevent or break up large mobs. These techniques, supplemented by the work of the Community Relations Board to try to calm the situation and initiate dialogue, proved relatively effective in limiting several subsequent disturbances. The police sought to quell future frustration before it spread.

The business community, however, sought to address what they perceived as the root cause: black economic deprivation. If blacks burned substantial portions of the community, it was because too many did not have a stake in it. Local government consultants' reports in 1981, 1989, and 1992 concluded that Miami's black communities most needed an economic lift (Ronnie Greene 1998a; Ronnie Greene 1998b). Given that these were business leaders, they did not see jobs for blacks as the fundamental problem. Instead, the scarcity of black businesses that could provide jobs for blacks was seen as the major cause of unemployment and alienation among blacks. Many looked back nostalgically to the days of segregation, when Miami's original black neighborhood, Overtown, contained a thriving business community that included not only retail stores but also a bustling nightlife with national headliners who performed after their engagements in Miami Beach (Dunn 1997). Moreover, had not the Cubans succeeded by starting up thousands of small businesses, despite the fact that many had arrived penniless and unable to speak the language? Many of the middle class blacks with whom the members of the business elite interacted supported the view of the problem as mainly one of economic development. The Civil Rights agenda of the 1960s and 1970s had broadened beyond civil and political rights to economic concerns. The specific focus on black entrepreneurial development reflected a broader national trend spawned by the "Reagan revolution," which emphasized encouraging private over public initiatives and which persisted through the 1990s.

Business leaders raised $5 million and organized a Business Assistance Center (BAC) to provide training, technical assistance, financing, and the facilities for "incubating" new businesses, including affordable office space and shared clerical staff. The sponsors of the BAC did not want to repeat the experience of public-sector programs with poor loan repayment records and high mortality rates among the start-ups. So they developed relatively stringent criteria to qualify candidates for loans. The City of Miami created Miami Capital, a lending arm focused on black neighborhoods. Miami-Dade Community College also established a branch in the largest black community, Liberty City, which focused on business development. Florida International University, part of the state university system, created a business development center that also focused on blacks. In 1998, after most of Miami's black neighborhoods received a federal designation as a federal enterprise zone, Miami-Dade County created a one-stop center designed to provide small-business owners and entrepreneurs with loans, business training, and development (Casimir 1998a).

Throughout the 1980s and 1990s, numerous banks announced plans to open branches in black communities and to provide a full range of services. The Metro-Miami Action Plan, an agency created by the county commission in the 1980s after the riots, pledged $250,000 to hire professional staffing for a credit union. Private banks had long ignored Miami's black neighborhoods. Miami's banks had the third-worst record in the nation, behind Los Angeles and Chicago, for investing in black neighborhoods (Semple 1995). In response to complaints of undeserving minorities and with the threat of fines from the federal Community Reinvestment Act, numerous banks announced black neighborhood initiatives. NationsBank teamed with the NAACP in 1994 on a $10 billion loan program in the southeastern United States, with a base just north of Miami in Fort Lauderdale. Barnett Bank announced it would open a full-service branch in Liberty City, the first bank branch opened in that community in ten years. First Union Bank announced it would provide low-income customers up to $100 million in home loans over the next three years and review claims of lending discrimination. A pilot program started by Sun Bank in Liberty City and South Dade enabled organizations such as churches to sponsor groups of businesspeople seeking loans of $500 to $5,000 (Barry 1994). People's National Bank, Florida's only African American-owned bank, similarly sought to serve Miami's black neighborhoods (Wilcox 1994). In 1998, a group of black businessmen took over Miami Ventures, which was created four years earlier by the Beacon Council with a $1.7 million grant to fund reconstruction in the wake of Hurricane Andrew. The fund invested exclusively in black-owned businesses.

The business community also encouraged affirmative action for businesses. In order to expand the black middle class, the main public sector entities—metropolitan Miami-Dade County, the City of Miami, the Dade County Public Schools—developed set-aside programs for black businesses, whether African American or newcomer black. When a Cuban-led snub of Nelson Mandela by public officials triggered a national black boycott of area tourism, civic leaders' response was not to welcome African leaders in Miami, but rather to promote black business in Miami. Organized by Miami lawyer H. T. Smith, the boycott lasted three years, and by the time it ended in May 1993, it had cost Miami an estimated $20 million in tourism, as two dozen meetings and 46,000 delegates bypassed the area. When they agreed to call off the boycott, local black leaders obtained promises that had nothing to do with civil rights or even the slight of Mandela. Rather, white American business leaders committed to a series of measures to ensure greater black participation in the area's tourism industry. Among the commitments were a black-owned convention hotel, scholarships for black students, incentives to keep black professionals in Miami, and increased capital for black-owned businesses (Pugh 1994; DuPont 1998). By 1999, the Greater Miami Convention and Visitors Bureau had made 115 scholarships to African Americans.[1] Ground was finally broken in 1998 for the black-owned hotel on Miami Beach. Increased capital came primarily from redirecting other sources, such as the state hurricane relief fund, which made $900,000 available for loans for black-owned businesses in hurricane-affected Dade County (Pugh 1994).

In 1994, Miami-Dade Public Schools committed itself to hiring only black contractors to rebuild the high school in the largest black neighborhood. Civic leaders also exhorted corporations to increase their purchases from black vendors. The host committee for the 1995 Super Bowl, which was held in Miami, strongly urged that National Football League contractors subcontract with minority businesses, and even created their own subcommittee to help them find minority subcontractors. About a dozen black firms obtained subcontracts.

White American businesses also actively sponsored some promising black entrepreneurs. In 1993 the Beacon Council, a local organization that conducts research on and promotes local business, created the Network 100, a list of the area's top one hundred black-owned enterprises, in an effort to raise their public profile. It then offered to nurture ten local black businesses with the intent of placing them among the top ten of black businesses in the country. Subsequently, two black-owned construction firms made it into the top ten black firms nationally. American white business and political leaders also reached out to established black professionals and executives to serve on boards and advise on racial problems.

Government-initiated community development corporations (CDCs) and redevelopment-revitalization plans sprouted up in every black neighborhood (Victor Greene 1968; Casimir 1998a; Casimir 1998b; Casimir 1998c). With great hopes for initiating neighborhood revival, a large black-owned department store opened in 1991 where the epicenter of the 1980 riot had been (Semple 1995). A few blocks away, the Tacolcy Economic Development Corporation led the most successful redevelopment. The 1980 riots resulted in the burning and looting of both of the major supermarkets in Liberty City and both decided not to rebuild. Liberty City was without a supermarket until Tacolcy, under the leadership of Otis Pitts, spearheaded the development of Edison Plaza, which contained a large chain grocery story, and the nearby Edison Towers, the first new housing project in Liberty City in twenty years (Whitefield 1998a). The efforts gained Pitts a MacArthur Fellowship, commonly known as a "genius" grant, and a position on a local bank's board of directors. In 1992 President Clinton placed him in charge of the federal government's rebuilding efforts following Hurricane Andrew while Pitts was deputy assistant secretary of the U. S. Department of Housing and Urban Development. Shortly after that project was completed, Pitts became an executive with the Codina Group, one of the largest and most important Latino development firms in the area. He then formed his own private corporation, which sought and obtained construction contracts from local government (Semple 1995; Fields 1998). He epitomized the personal and community development that local business leaders hoped to accomplish, but he was not the only one on whom effort was expended.

In early 1999 Miami-Dade was selected as a federal empowerment zone, which Penelas promised "would provide significant [financial] resources for inner-city economic revitalization." By mid-2000, there had been little to show for it. Federal money was nonexistent. Even more telling, Penelas was unable to secure any funding for the zone from the state during the legislative session.

The focus on economic development rather than the civil rights era emphasis on civil rights was reflected also among some African American leaders. Otis Pitts, a local African American entrepreneur who received a McArthur "genius" award, simply stated that the answer to the problems of the inner city was "to reintroduce market forces" (Fields 1998). Robert Steinback, an African American columnist in the *Miami Herald*, claimed, "I do see evidence that influential black Americans— perhaps exasperated with the rich and powerful who always manage to undermine (or take for themselves) any attempt at government assistance to the poor—increasingly are seeing the answer in capitalism. There is futility in asking others for help; there is empowerment in providing for oneself" (Steinback 1998).

Economic conditions for at least some African Americans undoubtedly improved in the 1980s and 1990s. Roughly, one in five black households in Miami-Dade had an income above $50,000. Approximately the same proportion were college graduates; one in six were in an occupation that would be considered professional or managerial (Fields 1995). The percentage of blacks in higher-paying professional, managerial, and technical jobs in the 1990s across the United States was unprecedented, and Miami-Dade was slightly above the national average (Charles and Morgan 1997). With about half of the state's estimated four hundred black physicians located in South Florida, the Florida Access Independent Physicians Association successfully helped black doctors break into managed care locally. South Florida also had overwhelmingly the largest black-owned businesses in the state, with over six times the revenues of

West Palm Beach, the Florida city with the next largest number of black businesses. Accordingly, the Miami-Dade Chamber of Commerce, south Florida's oldest black chamber of commerce, experienced fresh growth, with more than eight hundred members at the end of the 1990s and a budget over $425,000 (Garcia 1999).

There were also gains in political representation following the redistricting based on the 1990 census. Florida had twenty black members in the State House and three south Floridians as members of the U. S. Congress (Whitefield 1998b). Miami-Dade County government adopted single-member districts in the early 1990s, and the first chair of the new commission was an African American, Arthur Teele (Filkins 1993). In three municipalities just north of downtown Miami—El Portal, North Miami, and North Miami Beach—blacks gained positions on the city commissions in the mid-1990s. At the end of 1999, El Portal elected a Haitian majority to its city council, the first Haitian majority of any government in the United States.

Blacks also gained visible positions in local elite institutions. The Non-Group, originally created by the American white elite, in the late 1990s gained its first black co-chair, lawyer George Knox. Mr. Knox was also appointed to the state Work and Gain Economic Self-Sufficiency (WAGES) board charged with overseeing welfare reform. Another African American, James W. Bridges, became president of the Dade Medical Society. Albert Dotson Sr. chaired the Orange Bowl Committee, and another African American was its executive director (Pugh 1994; Wooldridge and Fields 1998). By the year 2000, the director of Miami's Urban League could conclude, "It's no longer a black-white theater. There have been four black chiefs of police since McDuffie. We have black judges all over the place. We have black lawyers, black state attorneys" (Whitefield 2000a).

In spite of all this apparent progress, there were just as many, if not more, pessimistic indicators. The 1980 riot spawned numerous redevelopment efforts that produced few visible benefits. President Jimmy Carter pledged to rebuild Liberty City, the most heavily damaged area, and about $116 million in federal money was promised for riot relief. But a 1985 General Accounting Office report said there was considerable confusion about federal commitments. Of the $70.6 million in federal funds actually spent, according to the U. S. General Accounting Office, only slightly over one-half went to communities affected by the rioting. Of the remaining money, some was used to help devastated businesses that decided to relocate outside of riot-torn areas, $1.9 million went to a job training center in a predominantly Cuban-American neighborhood, and a $500,000 grant went to refugees, not riot victims (Whitefield 2000a).

In 1998, it was revealed that $1 million budgeted for historically black Overtown had been diverted to subsidize a city-owned theater. The Miami city manager claimed that the community redevelopment organization in charge of Overtown that was created in the wake of the 1980 riots was "the most mismanaged organization in the city's history" (Casimir 1998c). "We've got a lot of shops that are just going by the skin of their teeth, and if they just had enough capital they could hire more local residents and expand," said McKinnon, executive director of the Naranja Princeton Community Development Corporation. Like others, he expressed optimism—but with an asterisk. "I can't help but be a little leery about the history of Dade County politics," he said. "Things start off with good plans, but one-third of the way through, new priorities take place" (Ronnie Greene 1998a).

Even in response to disasters, commonly referred to as equal opportunity tragedies, promises to black communities were less likely to be fulfilled. Blacks hit by Hurricane Andrew were more likely to be insured by smaller insurance companies, which were less likely to make satisfactory settlements. Blacks were also more likely to reside in smaller, unincorporated communities that offered no immediate local government assistance. The county, state and federal governments that were supposed to help them rebuild never delivered, according to local residents. Even unincorporated white areas were rebuilt more quickly. A public school in the hard-hit neighborhood of Country Walk was rebuilt almost immediately, whereas a school in the black neighborhood of Perrine had to wait two years (Peacock, Morrow, and Gladwin 1997).

Black businesses did grow, but many took hold outside of Miami's traditional black neighborhoods. Accordingly, a perception of black business decline remained because the number of black-owned businesses in black neighborhoods decreased. Yet black businesses struggled outside of the black community. In 1993, minority businesses complained that they were being forced out of the high-profile Bayside Marketplace managed by the Rouse Company, a development in which minorities had been promised space (Barciela 1993). In the mid 1990s, two Liberty City businesses that had been pointed to as signs of the black business success and that had received significant subsidies failed, first a grocery store and then a large discount store. George Knox, a prominent black attorney, pointed out that "Alonzo Mourning (the star center for Miami's professional basketball team) makes more per year than the fourth largest black-owned business in Florida grosses" (Whitefield 1998a). Similarly, in the mid 1990s the top Miami black-owned firm in terms of revenue (Toyota of Homestead) had lower revenues than the twenty-fifth Latino firm (Sedano's Supermarkets) (Semple 1995). And, while the number of Miami-Dade's black-owned businesses rose through the 1990s, the total with paid employees actually fell slightly (Ronnie Greene 1998a).

The various financial institutions also confronted difficulties. By 1990, almost two-thirds of the $560,000 loaned by Miami's Model City Small Development Program, designed to inject money into small Liberty City businesses, was in default (Whitefield 2000a). The rigid criteria for incubating new black businesses constructed by the Business Assistance Center (BAC) disqualified nearly all prospective black businesses. The BAC was forced to devote its resources almost exclusively to financing investments associated with minority set-aside governmental contracts (Semple 1995). People's National Bank of Commerce had become locally-owned and black-owned in 1983. In 1990, the bank failed to repay a $3.5 million loan from Miami-Dade County, which had tried to bail out the bank. A year later, the Federal Deposit Insurance Corporation took over the shares. Three prominent local black businessmen bought the institution from the FDIC in late 1992, with 25 percent of the $1.7 million purchase price financed by seven area banks and thrifts. It became one of only thirty-eight black-owned banks nationwide. It prospered for a few years but began to founder in the mid 1990s and appointed a new president, an African American from Louisville, to stem more than two years of losses (Cordle 1998). Shortly thereafter, the Comptroller of the Commerce seized People's National Bank. Its assets were sold to the Boston Bank of Commerce, and its former president assessed a civil fine of $2000. The firm, however, remained black-owned, although not locally-owned. In 2000, the bank formed a strategic alliance with Miami Ventures, a venture capital fund that targets black-owned firms, and became the first black-owned bank in the United States to provide both equity and debt financing (Cordle 2000).

In addition, in the late 1990s, the City of Miami took control of Miami Capital, its lending agency for black neighborhoods, after an internal audit revealed a high default rate along with one loan to someone who had a recent bankruptcy. At the same time, blacks in general had an extraordinarily difficult time obtaining mortgage loans. Through the 1990s, Florida's banks and thrifts had the nation's worst record for lending money in the low- and middle-income communities where they do business. In the mid 1990s blacks in south Florida were twice as likely as non-blacks to be turned down for a mortgage and the U. S. Justice Department was investigating Florida's largest bank, Barnett Bank, for alleged discrimination against black applicants. While Dade County as a whole had a home ownership rate 10 percent below the national average, the rate in twenty black neighborhoods was 50 percent below the norm, the report found.

Many, including some white Americans, responded cynically to the repeated promises of resources and redevelopment for Miami's black communities. The white American columnist for the *Miami Herald*, Harold Kleinberg, reflected that he had co-chaired a subcommittee in the late 1970s to redevelop Overtown, the black neighborhood next to downtown Miami. Little happened in the wake of that effort, and he expected little this time. He quoted the Miami Urban League Chairman, Willard T. Fair: "Nothing will happen in Overtown until such time as the establishment chooses to dismantle what is left of it and rebuild it as part of a larger downtown" (Kleinberg 1998).

Yvonne Edwards, a local black activist, affirmed, "There have been promises and promises and promises for thirty years. Quite frankly, the community is tired of promises" (Ronnie Greene 1998b). At a county commission meeting, African American county commissioner Barbara Carey waved a study by Florida International University that detailed how the construction of Interstate 95 carved up the historically black neighborhood of Overtown, destroying its integrity by directly displacing close to 12,000 residents, and indirectly another 4,830. She added that her own family had owned a business in the neighborhood that permanently closed because of the highway construction (Chardy 1998). When five hundred black community leaders met in 1998, they concluded that, in spite of many promises and plans, conditions had not significantly improved since the 1980 riots. Roy Phillips, president of Miami-Dade Community College's Homestead campus, asserted, "When the disturbances happen, the first thing we do is come up with a new plan. All we have to do is dust off the old plans and start over again" (Whitefield 1998b).

In spite of the evidence that the efforts to help blacks actually accomplished little, they still produced a backlash both locally and nationally. The refurbishing of a public high school under the school board's program had huge cost overruns ("The Northwestern Debacle" 1996; Mailander 1996). Latinos and women also felt they had been discriminated against and should be included in set-aside programs. Most importantly, however, white American contractors resented what they saw as reverse discrimination embodied in all minority set-aside programs. They sued and a U. S. District Court ordered a halt to the minority set-aside program. The Federal Court of Appeals and the U. S. Supreme Court in a separate but similar case subsequently upheld the decision (Tanfani 1996). The County rewrote their rules to make them race- and gender-neutral (Charles and Morgan 1997). Five years later, black construction contracts with the county had fallen from 10 percent to 4 percent (Doris 2000). Sherwood Dubose, executive director of the Metro-Miami Action Plan Trust, a multi-ethnic agency that promotes economic development in poor areas, commented, "The private sector does not do a lot of business with blacks. I would say most of the black businesses nationwide, if it were not for government contracts, would not have contracts" (Charles and Morgan 1997).

While the black middle and professional class appeared to be expanding, it was not growing very fast. In 1990, Miami and Fort Lauderdale combined had slightly fewer than fifty thousand black households making more than $35,000 annually. Atlanta had double that, and the Washington, D.C., area, three and one-half times that (Charles and Morgan 1997). Only 2.4 percent of Dade's black households had incomes of more than $75,000, compared to 5.4 percent of non-Hispanic whites and 3.5 percent of Hispanics, according to the 1990 census. No one from South Florida made *Black Enterprise* magazine's list of the forty highest-ranking businesses. There was no growth in the numbers of blacks on local boards. Of twenty-nine directors at Florida's two largest companies, Carnival Cruise Lines and Florida Power and Light, in 1997 there was only one black man (McQueen, Pugh, and Duhart 1993). While overall more blacks were in positions of power in the 1990s than ever before, they were still under-represented. Blacks represented slightly more than 20 percent of the county population, but held only about 10 percent of positions of power.[2] Because of the historically black Florida Memorial College, blacks appear to do well in the field of education. They come close in municipal government, where they hold 17 percent of positions that have decision-making power. They have virtually no presence as partners in Miami-Dade's largest law firms (Branch-Brioso 2000b). Adora Obi Nweze, president of the Miami-Dade branch of the NAACP, declared, "Things stand in pretty rough shape. After all these years of fighting and struggling, you would have thought we would have made some progress."

For the rest of black Miami, those who were not fortunate enough to be middle class, conditions were definitely worse. Overall, Miami-Dade has the sixth-highest poverty rate among major U. S. counties (Ronnie Greene 1998b). From 1980 to 1990, the poverty rate in the largest black neighborhood, Liberty City, actually increased, and the unemployment rate remained distressingly high—9 percent, well above the national rate of 3.9 percent. From 1990 to 1995, total jobs in the area dropped by 47.6 percent (Whitefield 2000a). Numerous studies based on the 1990 census revealed that Miami's blacks were at the bottom of the heap. The Children's Defense Fund calculated that Miami had the nation's second highest poverty rate for black children, 58.4 percent. A University of Michigan study placed the combined Miami-Fort Lauderdale urban area last of ten large metropolitan areas where two-thirds were poor or near-poor (McQueen, Pugh, and Duhart 1993). A Pittsburgh University analysis found black Miamians had the lowest standard of living (per capital personal income divided by the cost of living) in all of the nation's fifty largest cities (Pugh 1994).

Old-fashioned straightforward racism also burst forth periodically. When black candidates ran for local offices in the 1980s and 1990s, racist fliers mysteriously appeared on the doorsteps in non-black neighborhoods. During the same time period, blacks and Cubans would face off whenever a new city or county manager was to be appointed. Almost always, the Cubans won.

In 1998, the manager of a local Denny's locked the door when a group of six black and three white Florida highway patrol officers approached. He told them, "You guys don't look right." The officers said it was the second time they had been turned away from the restaurant. Ironically, in 1994 Denny's corporate headquarters had settled a class-action racial discrimination suit with black customers for $46 million. Since then, the company has done extensive anti-discrimination training nationally and has increased the diversity of its work force. The message apparently had not made it to Miami, although Denny's did immediately suspend the manager and apologized publicly (Brackey 1998). Less than a year later, a popular restaurant in Miami Beach run by an Asian immigrant added a 15 percent gratuity to the check of a black couple. Tips were voluntary at this restaurant, but the owner added this tip because, as he claimed to a Miami Beach policeman, "Blacks don't tip good." He later explained that he made the error because he "didn't speak English well." Ten years earlier, he had claimed to the *Miami Herald* that blacks "lacked the energy to work in the restaurant business" (Rabin 1999). These incidents are isolated, yet they assumed tremendous symbolic importance when they became publicly visible. Apparent attacks on black public officials also carried tremendous symbolic impact. Ever since the Civil Rights movement began, black county commissioners, a City of Miami commissioner, a Miami-Dade County school superintendent, and a state senator were indicted at the height of their careers (Colon 1998). While Latinos and others were also indicted for corruption, the impression remained among many that blacks were disproportionately targeted.

Jeb Bush, brother of soon-to-be president George W. Bush, further alienated Florida's blacks. Unlike any Florida Republican before him, Jeb Bush campaigned in black communities. He won 14 percent of the black vote in 1998, not overwhelming support but better than most Republican politicians ("If Bush Loses Race" 2000). When Jeb Bush became governor of Florida, however, he lost black support. He provoked a bitter controversy by instituting a program, the One Florida Initiative, that was supposed to be in blacks' interest but was created without any consultation with blacks. The initiative was to replace affirmative action for state university admissions with a race-neutral plan and to eliminate minority set-asides for contract work with the governor's office[3] (Bosquet 1999). The plan triggered a twenty-five-hour sit-in by two black state legislators and a march by thousands on the opening day of the state legislative session (Whitefield 2000b). Civil Rights groups also quickly formed a coalition, Floridians Representing Equity and Equality (FREE), a political action committee that includes the NAACP, the National Organization for Women, and the Hispanic Bar Association, which sought but failed to place a question on the November 2000 ballot asking voters to preserve affirmative action (Bennett 2000). The U. S. Commission on Civil Rights also condemned Bush's One Florida plan, calling it an "an unprovoked stealth acknowledgement that . . . segregation will never change" (Robinson 2000a). Governor Bush countered that the change promoted more minority business contracts, although black business owners maintained they actually lost business (Whitefield 2000b; Whitefield 2000c).

Prompted by the One Florida protests and the Elián affair, 135 of black Miami's elite bought a $9,500 advertisement in the *Miami Herald* in July 2000 that urged rejection of the "community's power paradigm" (by which they apparently meant the dominance of Miami Cuban and Anglo interests) and instead urged a focus on unity and the black community's concerns. They also stressed that blacks must share fairly in the economic wealth, and that all ethnic groups must fight for a fair and equal U. S. immigration policy for Haitians and other black people (Robinson and Acle 2000).

In response to local and state inattention to black affairs and in anticipation of the 2000 elections, many African Americans proclaimed, "We will remember in November." The November 2000 election not only focused national attention on Florida, but it also specifically highlighted blacks' frustrations and complaints. Black organizations organized vigorously and successfully got out the black vote. Blacks made up just 12 percent of Florida's population, but cast 16 percent of Florida's presidential vote, six points higher than in 1996. An estimated 93 percent voted for Gore and just 7 percent for Governor Jeb Bush's brother, George W. Bush ("If Bush Loses Race" 2000).

Yet thousands of votes from predominantly black precincts were apparently not counted. Longtime registered voters names were mysteriously omitted from voter rolls; people were prevented from voting because they didn't have photo identification; Haitian Americans were denied help from nearby Creole-language interpreters; and some regular polling places were closed, leaving voters perplexed as to where they should vote (Robinson 2000a). Historical memories of Jim Crow and the denial of the vote are not far beneath the surface in Florida, significant parts of which are similar to the Deep South. . The perception, perhaps the reality, that there had been a major disenfranchisement of black voters—by design, some charged—enraged large numbers of African Americans in Florida, who believed the election had been stolen. After the U. S. Supreme Court ruled in George W. Bush's favor on the potential recount of Florida's votes, Jesse Jackson proclaimed, "Dred Scott, Plessy vs. Ferguson and last week's decision have in common the disenfranchisement by appointed judges of African-Americans" (Reid 2000).

The U. S. Civil Rights Commission, the NAACP, and the congressional Black Caucus all conducted investigations into alleged disenfranchisement of black voters. The NAACP compiled three hundred pages of testimony, including claims of institutionalized racism (Hotchkin 2000; Andino 2001). Attention focused on a private Texas firm, with ties to a conservative group, that was hired to purge felons from the state's voter roles. In the process, they also purged eight thousand people who had only misdemeanors. Other blacks related that when they went to vote, they were told that they had requested absentee ballots and could not vote. Others talked of having to produce multiple pieces of identification, while whites did not (Weathersbee 2000). One out of ten votes in black precincts were discarded as compared to only one in thirty-eight in predominantly white precincts (Viglucci, Doughert, and Yardley 2000).

Mary Frances Berry, the chairwoman of the eight-member U. S. Civil Rights Commission, said the commission "had received troubling reports that there may have been some low moments in Florida on Nov. 7, 2000 . . . ranging from administrative inefficiency to intimidation and possible discrimination." Although the commission did not find evidence of conspiracy, at the end of a long day of hearings that included testimony from Governor Jeb Bush ("Little Evidence" 2001), commission members appeared frustrated by state officials—including Bush—who claimed that local authorities have control over Florida elections (Kam 2001).

Florida Democratic congressman Peter Deutsch asked, "If Florida was a foreign country and we had sent American election observers to Florida and we observed what happened in Florida—where 180,000 people's votes were thrown out, probably the majority of which were African-Americans'—is there anyone that would seriously think that the election in Florida was a legitimate election?" (Doyle 2001). Another Democratic state legislator, Jim Davis, announced, "The election was a terrible embarrassment to our state and voters" (Davies 2001). Even the relatively conservative British publication *The Economist* lamented, "It is bad that a country with such bleak memories of racism should find that it has so many faulty machines in black areas" ("The Myth of Perfect Democracy" 2000).

All of the hearings and media attention on the election did little to placate Florida's blacks. A poll three months after the election indicated that 91 percent of the blacks in Florida believed Al Gore won presidential election and the majority believe their ballots were unfairly rejected at a higher rate than those cast by voters of other races (Schroth and Associates 2001).

As the new millennium began, many of Miami's African Americans felt deeply alienated. Ray Fauntroy, president of the Miami-Dade chapter of the Southern Christian Leadership Conference, claimed, "I've lived here [in the Miami area] since December 1978. It's gotten a lot worse racially, in my opinion. For one, we have to speak Spanish to get work in the city of Miami and the county of Dade. And this is in America. There have been enough people brought to the country that have the jobs now, that the African American used to have and could have. But because No. 1, he doesn't speak Spanish, it's difficult to get the job. I would say that this aids and abets racism. Because it excludes me from work in my own community—in my own country. I cannot go to another country and take a job from an indigenous person. I can't go to

England and do that, I can't go to Cuba and do that, let alone force that" (Yearwood 1998).

THE WHITE AMERICAN
ELITE'S VIEW OF BLACKS

While African Americans express aggravation that they have been squeezed out of Miami's economy, white Americans proclaim frustration that nothing they do seems to make much difference for blacks. For all the frustration with the Miami Cubans, many in the white American elite view the "Cuban problem" as less severe and more transitional than the "black problem." A top civic leader stated, "The biggest problem in Miami is the plight of the blacks, who live in a condition of stark poverty, suffer from racism, have a high rate of teenage pregnancies. I don't see any hope. Money alone will not solve the problem, but the lack of it makes things even worse."

A newspaper executive was even more pessimistic: "There is a sense of hopelessness, nobody knows what to do. A sense of betrayal, that the millions of dollars which had been poured into the area had all gone for naught. On the one hand, it's easy to say people need more Hispanic leadership in solving inner city problems, but on the other hand, even if they were involved the problems are too great. The inner city where there is no family unity, no economy, just deplorable conditions, is tough for anyone to fight their way out. Desperately need to develop a middle class, more black leaders, and deal with jobs, housing, education, crime and drugs."

Miami Cubans' success provides a convenient and invidious comparison of how minorities can and should be. A banker asserted, "There are more black businesses than we have ever had, but there are not that many. Our experience has been disastrous. They come and go. And it seems like every time we find someone in that community that is doing well today, smother them with love and affection, we put them on a pedestal, they come to all the meetings, don't tend to business, and then fail. They employ relatives or friends only to have those people come in and steal from them, burn their property, things that are to you and me absolutely inconceivable. It's almost like the leadership in the black community—everyone that rises to the top seems to get knocked down somehow—one after the other. It's incredible. You contrast that with a Cuban, who takes his family and insists on education, helps them get a job, helps them get a second job, very successful."

Overall, Haitians in Miami fare worse than African Americans (Stepick 1996). Nevertheless, some white Americans perceive Haitians as better off. One businessman recounted that one can tell where Haitians live because there you see people going to the bank on payday to deposit their money. He implied the old racist stereotype that African Americans, seeking instant gratification, spend their money immediately. Another of Miami's most successful businessmen had a more social explanation: "I even have a theory that the black community is also accepted—basically what we have is the fear of poverty and they want to stay away from poverty—whether it's a white bum or a black bum—both are bums. But the moment you see a black who is well educated, well dressed, behaved, speaks well, I think he is accepted anywhere—and I really mean it—here in Miami, too. But there are too many blacks in poverty and it frightens people—the violence, the social unrest."

These perceptions, however, are not just idle musings. White Americans implement them in their businesses. The manager in charge of the main warehouse for a large retail chain said the reason blacks have a high rate of unemployment is that they have poor work habits. He maintained that Cubans from the Mariel boatlift, who came in 1980, have been largely absorbed in the labor market while blacks continued to have high unemployment because in his experience the latter were unreliable, contentious workers. The owner of a small industrial business explained differential employment rates by a somewhat more benign process. She explained that over the years her workforce had come to be mostly Latino where previously it had been largely black because the

Latino workers tended to stay on the job and recruit relatives and friends, whereas there was higher turnover among black workers.

The sense of pessimism among the white elite regarding blacks is fed by the scale of the problem. As one prominent American white businessmen concluded, "I think the approach in 1980 was wrong. They wanted to solve the problem with tokenism. You can't solve it with tokenism. I think they raised about five million dollars. That's a drop in the bucket. You need $500 to $700 million to succeed just in our little area."

Still, white American leaders were not willing to admit defeat, nor could they afford to. Although Latino political power was growing rapidly, it was still American whites who overwhelmingly controlled the largest private economic institutions in the city: department stores, banks, insurance companies, airlines, and fast food empires. Companies such as Ryder, Knight-Ridder, and Burger King had major stakes in Miami. Black leaders knew that, and repeatedly they chose to address their demands to the American white corporate leadership.

Not only did African Americans address white Americans, but they also preferred that Latinos not be part of the process. Many blacks felt that Latinos, specifically the Cubans, sought to claim a dubious minority status when it came to wresting benefits from the American whites, but hardly behaved like a minority when it came to attitudes and voting, or the exercise of power once they acquired it. Some blacks felt that any program that was not geared specifically to blacks would end up benefiting primarily Latinos. Through the 1980s, Miami Cubans were becoming the dominant group. By the 1990s, Miami Cubans clearly were part of the dominant political and economic group. Unlike many white American leaders, however, many of the Miami Cubans did not feel an obligation to facilitate black progress to compensate for past and present discrimination. The kinds of understandings and assumptions that many progressive white Americans had acquired over the decades through the legacy of the Civil Rights movement were not widely shared by Miami Cubans. Rather, many Miami Cubans saw their own history as proof that opportunities were available and that initial disadvantages, however real, could be overcome through hard work. Hadn't many Miami Cubans succeeded even though they started with no money and often no knowledge of English? Miami Cubans believed blacks had been dealt with very unfairly in the past, but felt that was no longer the case. Now they could study, go into business, and get ahead like everyone else, and if they did not it was their own fault. This was essentially what a substantial number of white Americans in the elite believed as well, but among the Miami Cubans this outlook was almost universal and more openly expressed. Not surprisingly, blacks were not eager to have Miami Cubans involved in efforts aimed at increasing opportunities.

When the Metro-Miami Action Plan (MMAP), a joint effort of Metropolitan Miami-Dade County and the City of Miami, with some support from the private sector, was created in the 1980s, it was not geared for poor people in general or minorities, but specifically for blacks. Consequently, Latino participation in MMAP was nearly nonexistent. Later efforts, such as Tools for Change, an organization to promote black economic development, were designed along the same racial lines.

Similarly, when blacks organized the Miami boycott in the wake of the snubbing of Nelson Mandela, Miami Cuban politicians were not even involved in the negotiations. The coalition of downtown businessmen that negotiated the end of the boycott included just a handful of Latinos. After the announcement that the boycott was over, some voices in the Miami Cuban community suggested that Miami-Dade's business leaders had bowed to pressure. Armando Perez Roura, general news director of Radio Mambi (WAQI-AM), described the boycott as "blackmail."

A few white American leaders wanted to expand the focus, to address directly the problem of social segregation and cultural conflict among not only blacks and whites, but also Latinos. Richard McEwen, then CEO of Burdines, a chain of upscale department stores, struggled to convince the white American business leadership as a whole that ethnic division was *the* major problem in Miami. The coincidence in 1980 of 125,000 Cubans arriving from the port of Mariel boatlift and the massive riot in black neighborhoods convinced McEwen that the problem of ethnic division involved both Latinos and black Americans, along with white Americans. When other white American leaders responded unenthusiastically, preferring to focus on integrating Latinos into white American organizations, while separately addressing the issues of black American frustration and poverty, he decided to start his own group. Greater Miami United was born as a "tri-ethnic" nonprofit group to promote ethnic understanding. It received moderate corporate financial support as long as McEwen chaired the organization, but it was never enthusiastically backed by the business elite. After McEwen retired and several corporate supporters went bankrupt, the organization survived for a few years mostly with public funds. Before folding in the 1990s, Greater Miami United helped spawn MMAP, which persisted through the 1990s and into the next century. Miami-Dade County provided most of its funding, while business leaders supported more in name than with resources. As mentioned above, however, MMAP was viewed as an initiative specifically for the black community. Moreover, it never had enough resources to mount any broad-based, serious initiatives. Rather, its yearly conferences repeatedly identified problems that it encouraged others to address. As long as there were no race riots, most white Americans, and even more most Cubans, were less concerned with these problems, which they perceived as primarily those of only one segment of the community, not theirs.

FUTURE CONVERGENCE AND SEPARATION

In the 1960s and 1970s, the American white elite's belief in the power of assimilation prompted them to simply ignore the Miami Cuban presence, to tolerate them, and patiently to await their Americanization. The newcomer Cubans were hardworking and educated, and the federal government helped support them. There were few complaints about use of public services or the taking of jobs.

The white American elite's patience, however, was not rewarded. Rather than assimilating, Miami Cubans began assuming power while still speaking with an accent. By the start of 1990s, it was clear that Miami Latinos—especially Cubans—were in the process of acquiring enormous power. By the turn of the century, Miami Latinos rivaled the demographic presence and political clout of blacks in cities such as Washington, D. C., the economic strength of Asians in some Pacific Rim cities, and the symbolic cohesion of gays and lesbians in San Francisco.

Latino advances presented enormous challenges to the white American elite. They wanted to maintain cultural and linguistic hegemony while ensuring a favorable business climate that was increasingly tropical and Latin. They recognized that the process not only challenged them but also frustrated African Americans, a frustration that periodically produced conflagrations that threatened the area's economy. The white American elite could no longer wait for the newcomer immigrants to assimilate, to become Americans just like everyone else. The American whites realized they had to change their own behavior. They had to initiate integration.

From the mid-1980s on, American white and Latino elites increasingly collaborated, trying to overcome the divisiveness of parallel and separate structures. The *Miami Herald* began to support the Miami Cubans' condemnations of Castro's Cuba. A leading Cuban American businessman who was a member of the Cuban American National Foundation and who also participated very actively in civic endeavors led by the American white business elite, claimed that a bargain had been struck between Cuban elites and American white elites. "They [the white Americans] don't care about foreign policy," he said, referring to American whites. Nevertheless, the American whites would go along with the Cuban American political agenda on Cuba if Cuban American business leaders would participate in American white-led local civic activities.

Unease, however, commonly suffused the collaboration. Liberals perceived the *Miami Herald* as having caved in to Miami Cubans' right-wing ideology while nativists detected cultural pandering. Meanwhile, Miami Cuban hardliners still complained about the *Herald*. They had long memories of the 1960s and 1970s when they believed the paper ignored human rights abuses in Cuba. They remembered the mid-1970s when the *Miami Herald* advocated the end of the refugee airlift and of 1980 when the paper called for a quick end to the Mariel boatlift, while the paper's coverage of the new arrivals helped paint the group in a very negative light. Moreover, the 1990s right-wing Miami Cubans felt the *Herald* went too far in advocating free speech for those who supported Castro's regime. Many Miami Cubans also felt the paper too often went out of its way to criticize exile leaders who should be supported and rewarded for their anti-Castro stance regardless of what else they did. Miami Cuban critics of the *Miami Herald* give the paper scant credit for the unprecedented moves it did make, the creation of a Spanish-language edition and its subsequent editorial freedom and focus on exile politics. They dismissed these changes as no more than a business move, an overdue and partial concession to reality. The moves certainly were rooted in the newspaper's desire to maintain their market, but they also had consequences that reflected Latinos' integration into and power within the local community.

American white and Latino elites have come to share important common interests that revolve around Miami's future economic growth, interests that require coordination between the increasingly large numbers of Latino business elites and predominantly American white economic elites. In the mid 1990s, Mayor Alex Penelas was able to overcome massive Latino voter opposition to the building of a sports arena for the Miami Heat professional basketball team, through a series of deft negotiations that led team owner Micky Arison to make substantial concessions. The facility would not have been approved by the voters without the strong backing of the most powerful Latino politician in Miami. The Elián affair of 2000 again raised issues that divided Latinos from everyone else. Penelas's broad political ambitions were severely damaged when he seemingly defied federal authorities. More fundamentally, Miami Cuban anti-Castro interests were undermined, as Elián was not only reunited with his father in Cuba, but also support for the Cuban embargo weakened so significantly that it was partially lifted. Once the Elián crisis receded, white and Latino economic elites returned to their convergent economic interests, but not without memories of resentment.

While the *Miami Herald* made an early special effort to reach out to Miami Cubans, the business community preferred to avoid directly confronting what they viewed as "divisive" ethnic issues, such as riots or massive refugee influxes. Instead, they concentrated on issues they understood, and which they thought everyone could agree on, such as the need to foster economic development, improve the city's reputation, and fight crime and drugs. They created specialized organizations for each of these particular problems, including Miami Citizens Against Crime, Miami's for Me (to improve the image of Miami), Homes for South Florida, and Greater Miami Neighborhoods (to increase and improve low income housing), the Miami Coalition Against Drugs and Business Against Drugs (initially known as BAD), and Tools for Change (to promote black business development), Partners for Progress (to assist black participation in the hospitality industry), and We Will Rebuild (in the aftermath of Hurricane Andrew). The lion's share of public sector dollars, however, went to organizations that most directly promoted business interests—the Beacon Council, charged with luring companies to Miami, and the Greater Miami Visitors and Convention Bureau, which focused on Miami's traditional central industry, tourism, and not its new focus of international trade.

American white elites tended to believe that racial and cultural issues would fade with economic development and assimilation. Their persistence was an uncomfortable reality. They insisted, however, that Miami was, or at least should be, one community united in its efforts to promote itself. Directly addressing race and ethnicity was viewed as inherently divisive, even if pitched as a way to overcome divisions. The white American elite, nevertheless, did respond, as Miami Cubans gradually challenged the white American elite's hegemony. Miami Cuban power meant that white American business organizations had to reach out to Miami Cubans rather than wait for the Miami Cubans to come to them. The *Miami Herald* led the transformation and was soon followed by all the leading elite organizations from the Greater Miami Chamber of Commerce to the Non-Group and the Orange Bowl Committee.

The convergence, however, was not complete. The corporate parent of the *Miami Herald*, the Knight Ridder Corporation, abandoned Miami for San Jose's Silicon Valley in the late 1990s. And the Elián Gonzalez affair revealed that deep rifts remained between Miami's Latinos and its white Americans.

For American blacks the problem was entirely different. They sought to attain an equality they had never had. As Latino and Caribbean immigrants poured into the city, Miami's African Americans hoped to prevent the prospect of a double (American whites and Latinos) or triple (the former plus black Caribbean immigrants) subordination. Race and class fundamentally structured relationships. While many white Cuban, economically successful immigrants broke into the local inner circles of power, the vast majority of American blacks remained on the outside, as they always have. Some African Americans did achieve success through the 1980s and 1990s. A few were asked into the white American elite organizations. A few were elected to political offices. And a few were successful entrepreneurs. Class did make a difference within the black community. Nevertheless, those successful blacks were exceptions.

Black and white American elites interacted substantially, sometimes in collaborative situations, other times in the context of resolving conflicts, but always within a context in which the American whites had the lion's share of the economic power. In some cases, the existence of the third party, the Latino-Cuban bloc, may have facilitated collaboration between American whites and blacks, and even led some to redraw their ingroup/outgroup map. Referring to American whites and blacks, an Anglo county employee who had a dim view of Miami Cubans affirmed, "We are all Americans. We all speak the same language."

Black and Latino elites generally had more limited, and more con-
flict-laden, interactions. If the one case in which the two groups coa-
lesced and achieved positive results is an indication—namely, the challenge of the county's at-large electoral system— collaboration is most
likely in situations in which working together can achieve gains for both
groups, gains that cannot be attained by working separately. While
large-scale immigration had become a standard feature of many American urban areas by the 1990s, Miami is the only American metropolis in
which the newcomers were well on their way to becoming an establishment in a single generation. For working-class people, relationships
proceeded very differently.

THREE

Working in the USA
Ethnic Segregation and
Bureaucratizing Interaction

What they gave me was a desk and a test, and they told me that the test would cost me twenty or twenty-five dollars. I paid the twenty or twenty-five dollars, but did not pass the test because number one, I did not read English, I had problems with the language; and number two, the type of test they can give you . . . are so that one will not pass it. Three weeks after . . . there were ads in the newspapers . . . looking for people. I returned. They gave me a little better attention this time, did not give me the test, but they did not let me get in, either. I got in on the third time because my [American white] father-in-law was a member of a local and had become a friend of the local representative. I came in recommended by him and the business agent helped me to pass the test and I started working. (Pepe, a Cuban immigrant)

During the presidential election, in the midst of a political discussion among construction workers, a white American declared, "You guys [the immigrant workers at the construction site] are such assholes. Don't you know that they [the politicians] are all crooks?" An immigrant Haitian retorted, "Hey man, you mean you're not going to vote. Are you an American or what?"

The "chopper" sews as it cuts, they said. Until I saw it work, I was completely baffled by the apparent paradox. First, I had to learn how to thread the machine, by watching her, then by doing it myself over and over again several times. Then she showed me the way to put the piece in the jacket. I had a terrible time the entire day getting control over the foot pedal. All of the jokes from everyone not to get my fingers sewn together and not to get my fingers under any needles really weren't funny today. It's totally nerve-wracking. My shoulders are aching—and so is my ass from sitting on this hard chair the whole day. (Aline, an American white researcher and apparel worker)

These stories reveal tips of icebergs, small vignettes that when repeated daily combine to form a complete picture of newcomer immigrant and American workers in Miami-Dade County. In the first quote, Pepe, a carpenter by trade and a labor leader by conviction, received a rough reception when he arrived from Cuba ready to work in the United States. Pepe did not bring over any particularly nasty stereotypes about unions and their purposes. Instead, he considered unions to be benevolent organizations designed to help workers in their times of need. His rejection by the carpenters' union surprised, but did not defeat him. Labor unions in the United States, say what you will about their economic functions, have served for generations as voices for the disenfranchised. Yet, as in the case of Pepe and of other minorities, some unions have behaved in a less than exemplary manner. Inside many unions, the issues associated with the inclusion or exclusion of immigrants often create conflict within an organization. The gauntlet that confronted Pepe in entering the hiring hall may form part of this continuing conflict, but to him it represented something simpler. It was an exercise in power that resulted in the domination of one group (white Americans) over another (Miami Cubans). He was excluded as a Miami Cuban and had to rely on the power of a white American to get him incorporated into the organization. Eventually Pepe was included, just as many other Miami Cubans managed to be included into organizations from banks to universities.

As he rose through the organization, he remembered his first experience. Once in a position of power, Pepe proceeded to use it on behalf of those who had been victims of domination. Pepe began to rebuild the union by bringing in newcomers from all over Latin America. "The way that I see it, it is my job to give Latins a chance. If you are no good, you won't stay long, but I will always give a Latin a chance to prove himself." Pepe eventually became president of the local of the International Brotherhood of Carpenters and Joiners and today is one of the four regional representatives of the union, the highest ranking Latino in the International Brotherhood of Carpenters and Joiners, responsible for the entire southeastern portion of the United States.

The second quote, by an American white construction worker, reflects how newcomer immigrants can embody and even reinvigorate American values. The newcomer immigrants are often less cynical politically and express a more profound, sincere appreciation of America than those who think they are the real Americans.

The third vignette, from an apparel factory trainee, also represents an important element of immigrant work in Miami. It reminds us that the work of immigrants is not that different from the work the rest of us do. Immigrants in Miami are as controlled and directed by machines and by the rules and regulations of bureaucracy as any of us. These machines and routines define much of the immigrants' lives as workers and their process of Americanization. The rhythms of work drive individuals apart and together, sometimes resulting in conflict or competition, other times in solidarity and cooperation.

Latinos, Haitian immigrants, African Americans, and white Americans interact at work much as they interact outside of work. Sometimes they compete for rewards and resources. Other times they cooperate. They might cry or celebrate together or remain apart for a variety of reasons. At times, the geography of work, just like that of a large city, segregates them and limits their interactions. In other situations, they might be forcefully brought together, bringing out anger and frustration otherwise hidden. Diversity dominates the workplace. Sometimes it is celebrated; just as frequently, if not more so, workers and managers resist diversity. We focus on three different kinds of workplaces: an apparel plant with primarily women Latino workers, hotels and restaurants with a mix of newcomers and Americans, and unionized construction workers, particularly carpenters who were primarily established resident whites and Latinos. Besides the obvious diversity in who the workers were and where they worked, three important dimensions of diversity emerged in the research: the control of the workplace, patterns of conflict, and forms of cooperation.

THE DIVERSITY OF CONTROL

Years after Mr. Elman sold the apparel plant, his workers still talked about him. He cared, took the time. He was an accessible man who knew the names of all his employees, who cared if one was sick, who would always keep his door open to each worker directly, whom all could talk to and who attended to his workers' concerns beyond the workplace. As the Miami Cuban production control manager put it, "Mr. Elman knew the names of all the workers. He talked to every new [employee]. . . . People worked because they wanted to protect him." Nearly all the workers were Latinas, primarily Cubans. Mr. Elman was Jewish American, but the workers accepted him as one of their own, as the type of manager they loved to work for.

Mr. Elman effectively adapted his management style to his workers, thus reducing the importance of ethnicity and eliciting both loyalty and production from his workers. He elevated paternalism to an art form, not only calling everyone by his or her first name, but also remembering birthdays and asking about the welfare of children far and wide. The plant was unionized, but the union had little responsibility. If workers had a problem, they walked directly into the owner-manager's office to deal with it. Neither the union representative nor the supervisors played a mediating role in disputes. Mr. Elman exercised final and arbitrary authority, but he constrained himself with an implicit understanding of the rights and obligations of his workers.[1]

Elman's managerial style worked so well that he even convinced workers to gladly accept pay cuts. After the termination of a particularly important Sears contract in 1980, the plant struggled for a year with numerous small contracts. In 1981 it appeared as if his magic had been exhausted and the plant would have to close. Mr. Elman addressed the workers and managers with a recommendation that they work without benefits until things improved. In an emotional appeal from the steps leading to the production floor, in what might be his finest moment as a paternalistic owner-manager, he informed the workers that they had a choice. They could go home, he would pay their benefits for the current period and the plant would close indefinitely until new contracts could be established or, if the workers agreed to work without benefits for an undisclosed amount of time, the plant could continue to operate. He put the issue to a vote, vowing to comply with the voice of the majority. With the union's approval, all employees, including non-union management employees, voted on the issue. With only twelve opposing votes, the employees voted to work without benefits.

Mr. Elman's paternalistic democracy dissolved when a major American clothing manufacturer bought the plant in the mid-1980s. New management insisted on American, scientific management principles. Everyone would be treated equally and fairly. Rules were established and followed. Exceptions were not allowed, and if one had a complaint one took it to the union, not directly to management. They did not want the work process to be disrupted by employees running off the production floor into the plant manager's office.

In the interest of "improving working conditions," the new management announced policies that reduced the individualism expressed by the workers during work hours. Individual fans and radios were replaced by plant-wide air conditioning and piped-in music. Neither hot plates nor snacks were allowed beside the machines. Instead, the company put a new microwave in the lunchroom and encouraged its use during breaks. According to the workers, the plant had become Americanized.

The Americanization plan failed miserably. After the management change, the apparel plant's production declined and never recovered. Following five years of struggle, the manufacturer gave up and sold the plant. The managers brought down from company headquarters who instilled the American style interpreted their difficulties in terms of ethnicity and culture. They had worked previously in various American plants. According to the quality control manager, "The people [at other plants] are more easy to control than here." The managers concluded that they had imposed their northern, Anglo management techniques too quickly and brusquely upon an immigrant work force that had been accustomed to and worked well under the more paternalistic, less bureaucratic approach of the previous owner. The local top manager, an established resident white brought to Miami by the company, remains convinced that things would be better overall if the Latinos and Haitian immigrants became more like Americans rather than continuing to express the cultural identities permitted under a more paternalistic management style. The few Latino managers, all local Miami residents who worked under Mr. Elman, believe that the white Americans made mistakes in restructuring the work relations at the plant but also that over time the imported managers changed and became a lot more like the Latinos. The plant manager at least had learned to talk to people at all levels to get them to work for him, rather than just tacking a memo on the bulletin board. During his first year, he seldom communicated with the workers and took little advice from the older, newcomer Latino middle management group. As a result, according to the Chicago-based executive vice president, workers consciously resisted change by work slow-downs, eventually forcing the plant to close.

In contrast, the hotels and associated restaurants and the unionized construction site we studied began with and maintained an American-style organization of work. The hotels and restaurants were part of large national hotel chains, and as far as the workers could remember, their management had always been American, always hierarchical, run by strict rules, and impersonally striving for efficiency. Jobs were highly compartmentalized, with each department assigned specialized tasks that rarely brought workers from different job areas together. Tasks were notoriously routinized and labor-intensive. Workers viewed the time card as a weapon of management, and employees waited to clock in and out exactly on the minute. Regardless of the job, management expected every employee to be fully occupied except during breaks. Any infraction normally received some disciplinary measure, such as a warning, a write-up, or outright dismissal. To look occupied, employees busied themselves, even if they were doing nothing useful. Hafidh, a Kenyan research assistant who worked as a waiter in an airport hotel, reported, "Hotel work is boring, routine, stressful, physically and mentally demanding, and has few rewards in terms of wages, promotion, and job security." As a result, employees seldom worked for long, in contrast to the dedicated workforce that characterized the apparel plant. Instead, worker alienation from management suffused the hotels and restaurants.

While the organization charts of the hotels and restaurants clearly delineated hierarchical authority, workers often ignored their formal roles. A supervisor, such as a chef, has by designation more responsibilities and therefore authority over a cook. A cook, in turn, is higher than a server, and a server is over a busperson or dishwasher. Yet no one ordered or assigned work to anyone formally below, except through threat or intimidation. Workers simply refused to obey other workers, and they were even reticent to obey management. For example, a newcomer Cuban chef who had been at the hotel for about a year and a newcomer Puerto Rican cook who had been at the hotel for about ten years were always quarreling. After the cook's work schedule had been changed, he accused the chef of "being good for nothing." In response, the chef demanded that the cook be fired or he himself would leave. The cook was not fired. Instead, a month later he was transferred to a sister hotel in Boston at his own request. Another month later, the chef was fired, apparently because of an undue rise in hotel food costs. But soon after, the

American white food and beverage manager was heard saying that he did not need vocational school-trained chefs anyway. Informally trained and presumably less expensive chefs would henceforth suffice.

On another occasion, a newcomer Bolivian cashier asked a newcomer Cuban room service waiter to help in the restaurant during a particularly busy rush hour. The room service waiter refused. The American restaurant manager then ordered room service temporarily closed so that the room service waiter could help in the restaurant. The move infuriated the room service waiter. He pointedly stated that he was not there to work for others; he was there to make money. The newcomer-American divide was irrelevant to these disputes. Workers refused to obey other workers and only reluctantly responded to management, regardless of ethnicity or newcomer-American status.

Construction workers are far more autonomous. Owning their tools, construction workers are freed from the technological dependence found in occupations alienated from the means of production.[2] Construction workers defy management control and they get away with it. Mark, an American white supervisor, wanted Willie, a white American carpenter, to build a soffit (the underside of an enclosure to conceal air-conditioning duct work) with a two-foot span between the studs that framed it. Willie thought that a two-foot span was unsafe and directly told the supervisor that he would not build it to those dimensions. Mark meekly conceded and indicated that Willie could build it as he saw fit.

Another time, Alejandro, a Cuban carpenter in his fifties, had been working alone, about a hundred feet from the ground, framing the sides where the ceiling met the walls. To reach the third-story scaffold, he had to carry ten-foot studs in one hand up a ladder. At about 2:00 p.m., Steve, our researcher, noticed that Alejandro was visibly upset, sweating and shaking his head as if it ached. Just then, Danny, an American white supervisor, walked up, put his arm around Alejandro's neck, and asked what was wrong. Alejandro responded in English: "Danny, you know I am a good worker. I do what you tell me. But now, I have to say something. That scaffolding is dangerous. I can't work up there alone. How do you expect me to carry materials up there and do my job? I need someone to help me. Get me someone quick or else I am leaving. This job ain't worth dying for. You guys are the ones that talk about safety. It's in the contract. This is bullshit!"

Newcomers have penetrated all the industries that we investigated—apparel, construction, and hotels and restaurants. Their impact has not been uniform, however. In the apparel plant, an astute American owner-manager, the Jewish American, adapted to the newcomers with paternalism that engendered both loyalty and production. Subsequent owners and their managers, white Americans from the Midwest, attempted and failed to convert the workers to American management styles. The construction, hotel, and restaurant industries had no difficulty in assimilating workers into American management structures. The nature of American management structure, nevertheless, varied dramatically between the two industries, with hotels and restaurants demanding worker compliance with numerous detailed rules and regulations while construction workers exercised extraordinary autonomy in their jobs. Construction workers could defy management and get away with it, whereas the hotel and restaurant workers could defy coworkers but not management. In short, becoming an American worker is not the same for everybody. The diversity of the American workplace reflects the diversity of management structures as much as it reflects the diversity of people working within those structures.

CONFLICT AND DIVERSITY

Jean, a newcomer Haitian bundle boy in his thirties, grabbed a bundle of material from the hands of an older Miami Cuban woman, Angelina. Jean's job was to lighten the load on the seamstresses by carrying bundles to their machines for them. Jean further assumed the responsibilities of trying to even out the good bundles, those that were easier to sew and thus could be finished more quickly. From Jean's perspective, Angelina had unfairly taken a good bundle. The two engaged in a shouting match and were referred to the plant manager's office. The plant manager first met with Jean and told him that he should not and could not take bundles out of people's arms. The plant manager also admitted that he believed that Angelina purposefully tried to aggravate Jean. The plant manager then met with Jean and Angelina together. Angelina began "freaking out" because she thought she was being blamed for Jean's pulling the bundle from her hands. Finally, the manager indicated that if it happened again, they would both be fired. Angelina then asked to meet with the manager alone, apparently because she thought it was unfair that he had a meeting alone with Jean. In this last meeting she said, "If you don't want me, why not fire me!" While the plant manager believes that there are fewer such disputes in the Miami plant than in other plants within the corporation, he is certain that the incidents that do occur escalate to "big deals" much more often due to the ethnic nature of the conflicts.

Sam, an African-American cook, and Memo, a Latin pre-cook, quarreled when Memo insisted that he did not understand Sam's shouted instructions. A few minutes later, after tempers had cooled, Sam informed Hafidh, our newcomer Kenyan server-researcher, "The Spanish have taken over everything in Miami. And now they want to impose their language." Hafidh gently replied, "Say, Sam, you were really harsh on Memo, what if he truly did not follow what you were saying?" "I don't care. The guy is pretending. How does he talk to the chef in English? Besides, what I wanted him to bring out from the freezer is stuff he always handles and knows. Hey, this is the U. S. A.! When you come here, it is English!"

Both of these examples reflect conflicts intrinsic to the work, but with an ethnic tinge. As the apparel manager explained, conflicts over bundles exist in all the company's plants, regardless of the ethnicity of the plant's workers. Similarly, kitchen conflicts constantly boil over when workers fight to keep up during peak periods. Yet in the above examples and throughout Miami, conflict that would happen regardless of the participants' immigrant or American background becomes interpreted as ethnic or newcomer-American conflict. Angelina always wants the good bundles, but she also consistently nags Jean, the Miami Haitian bundle boy. Similarly, Sam and other cooks frequently have difficulty communicating clearly in hot, crowded, busy kitchens. But Memo's limited English particularly aggravates Sam. Occasionally ethnicity motivates the conflict, and language is commonly the flash point. During rush periods, servers frequently scrawl, misspell, or fail to use accepted menu acronyms, thus confusing cooks and delaying orders. Servers insistently urge the cooks to hurry up, complaining to each other, "What a pain, what a slow cook." The cook retorts, "Write English," or "Better get back to school," "This is not Haiti," "Where are you fellas from?"

LANGUAGE AND CONFLICT

With a 1980 anti-bilingual county referendum, South Florida spawned the contemporary language restriction movement in the United States, which produced fifteen English-only laws or amendments to state constitutions during the 1980s (Castro, Haun, and Roca 1990; Castro 1992; Tatalovich 1995). Language is a metaphor, an emotionally charged emblem of identity and power that easily antagonizes Americans. At one construction site, managers posted a sign inside their office declaring that all telephone conversations must be held in English. At another site, two Latin sheet rockers were applying sheeting to the studs with three-quarter-inch screws. The supervisor, Dan, came up to them after they had spanned half of a hundred-foot wall and told them to use one-inch screws. Despite his efforts at using sign language, Dan could not get his point across. His face became red with frustration, and he shouted that everyone should have to understand English if they wanted to work there. Finally, Ed, a bilingual carpenter, intervened and translated Dan's orders. The sheet rockers understood and began taking down the sheeting. Dan thanked Ed and left.

The carpenters' resolution of the language problem contrasts with

English Only advocates and other cultural conservatives' view that immigrants, specifically Latino immigrants, resist speaking English and maintain Spanish through loyalty to their home culture rather than American culture. Newcomers in the workplace unequivocally recognize the importance of English. Joseph, a Haitian carpenter who spoke perfect English, noted, "If you speak the language, that's your first step to making it. You can't advance without knowing the language." Virtually all construction workers understood and spoke enough English to get along, although they spoke among themselves in their native languages. A white American business agent for the carpenters union, David, conjectured that language was not as much a problem in construction-related industries because the workers know a specific trade or craft; it is their skill that earns them money.

Moreover, language in and of itself does not cause conflict. The inability to communicate one's needs and intentions does. At a work site, if one can find a common language cooperation usually follows and the potential for hostilities and tensions is reduced. Miami Cuban carpenters unable to find the right word in English frequently use gestures to indicate the tool and receive it from American white coworkers.

Spanish has penetrated so deeply among all workers that being monolingual in Spanish is seldom an obstacle, especially for relations among coworkers within the carpenters union. While walking to the third-story bay windows, Steve noticed Frank, a white American, address Alberto, an older Miami Cuban sheet rocker, in Spanish: "Hey *joven!*" Alberto responded in English, "Hey Frankie." A few minutes later, Alberto was hugging another American white carpenter, saying in English, "How's the kids?" The white American responded in English, "They're fine, buddy. How's Marie?" At a lunch break, seven Miami Cubans and one American white were eating together. They were all talking, primarily in Spanish, about the white American's girlfriend, as one of the bilingual Miami Cubans simultaneously translated for the American white.

Miami Haitians are even more likely to engage in multilingual conversation. Haitian Creole is spoken solely among native speakers. Miami Haitians have responded to this reality by learning both English and Spanish. Daniel, a Miami Haitian Laborers Union foreman, would give instructions to Miami Haitian laborers in Creole. But to the older Miami Cuban carpenters, he spoke Spanish, while he spoke English to American whites, including the supervisors. One day, Alberto, a Miami Cuban, walked up to an unknown Miami Haitian laborer and put his arm around him. The Miami Haitian responded in Spanish, "*Que pasa, man?*"

Still, language can cause a chasm between members of different ethnic groups. An American white carpenter put it to a Miami Cuban coworker, "Just shut up. I can't understand a word you're saying." For many Americans, both black and white, language is simply a part of what they see as the problem. "When the union went Cuban, that was the end for us. The wages went down, contractors started hiring all those illegals. We lost control over our union." It is indeed true that at the time of his statement the carpenters union had a newcomer Latino president who had aggressively recruited Latinos into the organization. Soon after, a newly elected union president, an American white, dispatched two of the high-ranking Miami Cubans to Tampa so they could learn some "humility."

Not only do American institutions, such as unions, contain contradictions in their behavior toward newcomers, but individuals frequently express contradictory attitudes and behaviors. A female white American waitress claimed there were "too many Latin people in Miami." Yet her next-door neighbors are Miami Cubans, and she did not mind them. Her son-in-law was also a Miami Cuban, but she defended him by stating that he hardly spoke any Spanish.

Language has become a potent symbol of emotions and power relations. In mundane, day-to-day relationships, Americans and newcomers can overcome language differences, but language differences still carry emotion and reflect unequal power relationships, as revealed in the generation gap between Latinos. Younger, bilingual Miami Cubans frequently use English as a mark of authority and status over older Miami Cubans, who only speak Spanish. One day, for example, when Steve was working with Fred and Ignacio, Alberto, an older, nearly monolingual Spanish-speaker, asked in Spanish for advice about framing a wall on the second floor. Fred and Ignacio, younger, English-dominant Cubans, gave him their opinions, but they did so in English.

RACIAL DIFFERENCES

The English-only xenophobia, however, is frequently submerged by racism. For construction workers, the unionized laborers are the lowest skilled, lowest paid, and least respected. Not coincidentally, laborers are exclusively black, containing a mix of African Americans and newcomer Haitians. On the other end of the scale, those trades that require state licensing, such as electricians and plumbers, have the highest prestige, are virtually all white, and have been the slowest to admit Latinos, let alone blacks. On one occasion, an African American laborer broke the golden rule of construction work culture. He "messed with another worker's equipment," not just the equipment of another construction worker, but of a high-status white American duct worker. The American white was furious. He came to researcher–construction worker Steve and asked if he had seen anyone take his equipment. Steve responded, "No," and the duct worker left screaming, "That son of a bitch. That fucking nigger" (Morris 1989).

The importance of race emerged more subtly in how construction workers related to supervisors. Miami Haitians and African Americans were the most respectful and careful with supervisors. They usually did not speak with supervisors or even other workers, except when it related directly to work. For example, Don, a white American supervisor, told Daniel, a Miami Haitian laborer, to get studs for Domingo and Steve. Daniel responded with a nod and "OK"; he never questioned what size studs or the safety of moving them or indicated that he was in the middle of doing something else. Never once did we observe African Americans publicly question management's rules about safety or anything else.

The combination of racism and xenophobia hit newcomer Haitians especially hard. A newcomer Latino supervisor in the apparel plant claimed that newcomer Cuban apparel workers made it clear to the Miami Haitian workers and the supervisors that they should be given "preference in everything" because of their seniority (since virtually all started working at the plant before the Haitian immigrants), that is, they should get the best work, the best bundles. "If it was a slow day with not enough work, the Cubans felt that they should go home last."

Anti-Haitian prejudice also emerged in the restaurants. Almost immediately after arriving in mid-1991, a new management team at the seafood restaurant announced a set of cost-saving measures, including reduced hours. Nearly everyone suffered, but Haitian immigrants seemed to have their hours reduced more. One newcomer Haitian worker, Lucy, complained, "How am I supposed to feed my children?" Management responded that workers not willing to conform to the changes should feel free to leave and look for another job. After being commanded to leave work early three times, even before putting in her reduced hours, Lucy ignored the order and continued scooping lettuce out of the bin and filling bowls with salad. Vance, the new white American manager, confronted her, looking her in the face and demanding loudly, "Punch out immediately!" Lucy later claimed Vance's "having no respect made me crazy." She erupted verbally as best she could in English, telling Vance that he was no good, had no respect for Haitians, and only wanted white people working in the restaurant. While Lucy was the only one to publicly make these claims, other Haitian immigrants working there concurred under their breath.

Ethnic conflict seemingly suffuses some Miami work sites. Yet most of that conflict is not fundamentally ethnic or based upon newcomer-American prejudices. Rather, many places where Americans work engender conflict through the very process of working, regardless of who the workers are. In Miami and other places with significant numbers of newcomers, however, workers, managers, and others frequently interpret this conflict as a result of immigration or, more specifically, individuals' ethnic backgrounds. Moreover, language is not necessarily an especially difficult practical problem in the workplace, but it is often a potent symbol. Workers use language differences as emblematic of their frustration and occasionally both Americans and newcomers use language to maintain power over others.

These misinterpretations of the importance of newcomer status and language occasionally escalate conflict. As the American white apparel plant manager indicated, all apparel plants have conflicts, but in Miami they're a bigger deal. Being a black immigrant, specifically a Haitian, makes it an even a bigger deal. Throughout our work sites, blacks fared worse and Haitians fared the worst of all. Becoming an American worker includes expressing prejudices toward blacks.

COOPERATION AND SOLIDARITY

> "They [the owners] wouldn't even let me go through the front door. Once we bust our balls and finish a building, the guys who own it think we are not good enough to walk in the front door. People might see us or something. What bullshit! They even told us we would get fired if we did."
>
> —*A newcomer Haitian carpenter who had helped build a luxury hotel*

All the workers expressed some form of class solidarity, arguing that they knew how to run the business better than management and that they had to stick together to protect themselves from management. Hotel and restaurant workers generally viewed management as incompetent and incapable of doing the "real work" that staff does. At a luxury hotel on Miami Beach, one worker responded to a rumor that the hotel was being sold by stating, "It doesn't matter. . . . We do all the work here anyway. . . . Who cares what bank owns the hotel?" On an especially busy morning in an airport hotel, when Mark, the restaurant supervisor, arrived, he noticed that Diana, a white American server, had not yet put on her bow tie, and he severely reprimanded her. Later, when the restaurant had become extraordinarily busy, Diana complained,

> Christ! Why do they [management] always pick on us for small things like bow ties and stuff instead of like right now? Christ! These people [management] never let off. As long as they are around here, why the hell don't they let us do what we are supposed to? And they do their work, which is never much anyway. If you only know how I feel. There are times I never want to come back to this hole of a place. You hardly do anything without one of them picking on you.

Restaurant workers most commonly resisted management by conspiring to get a bit of a break from their work. Sometimes workers helped each other in routine tasks, acted as "lookouts" while others took a break during slow periods, covered for each other when someone was absent or late, and sympathized with a coworker in a stressful or traumatic situation. Demaris, a server, might say to her coserver, Janet, "I can't stand it anymore. I have to run to the ladies'. Please see to my customers." Or, "Will you do me a favor? Give me a hand here. Hold that door for me. I can't handle this alone." Or, "Refill that customer's cup over there. I have to run back to the kitchen."

Jim, the white American carpenters union steward, found himself battling both management and the union as he tried to protect a young Nicaraguan immigrant who had been working as a sheet rocker for four years, having been paid as a journeyman the last two years. When the subcontractor found out how young the Nicaraguan immigrant was and that he had not passed the apprenticeship program, he wanted to reduce him to apprentice wages. The Nicaraguan immigrant spoke little English and could not understand what the supervisor was saying to him.

When Ignacio, a bilingual Miami Cuban carpenter translated, the Nicaraguan immigrant threatened to walk off the job.

Jim, the white American, claimed, "They're really trying to fuck that kid. Look at this kid. He's getting screwed. He's got a family to support. That's the problem we got down at the hall; we got a bunch of chicken shits who are afraid to stand up for what is right." Later the same morning, addressing Dan, the supervisor, Jim asserted,

> Hey, Danny, this kid's been working for you for about a year now. All that time he was getting paid journeyman's scale. He's doing good work. So what's this shit that you're trying to pull? I know it's the [union] hall's fault, too. They fucked up. They couldn't even get the kid's work status right. But shit, just because the system's a pile of shit doesn't mean this kid should get the shaft. It really burns me up. The hall is so full of shit. Shit, you don't need to be an apprentice for four years before you start putting up rock. You can learn that shit in a few months. I bet none of these guys [other Latin sheet rockers] ever worked for such shit wages.

Carpenters extended their anti-management sentiments to union bureaucrats. Jack, a white American, the carpenters union steward, proclaimed, "We should start a civil case against the union for violating our contract. The members didn't want to take a wage cut, but we got it anyway. Shit, you can't take your grievances to the contractor or you get on the shit list. The union doesn't do shit about this. We fucked ourselves in a lot of ways. We gave away our bargaining power—the right to strike." Jim, another white American carpenter, added, "The union is just going downhill. . . . Reps are only in it for themselves. They only care about securing their own ass. That's the only incentive they have to protect the union. They protect the union, they guarantee themselves a job." Jack added, "They want what we want, but they're not on our side. When are you guys gonna face that fact? They're not working with us. They're working against us." Bill, another American white, declared, "You got that right. I'll tell you what. I'm sick of this shit. If they negotiate us out of one more benefit, I'm out of here." Mark, an older white American, shook his head and insisted, "Come on, guy. You're an old-timer just like me. We're both lifers. We'll be buried with hammer in hand."

Workers even more commonly achieve solidarity across newcomer-American lines in response to events that everyone experiences, what anthropologists call life-cycle rituals, such as birthdays, wedding and baby showers, and funerals, along with serious accidents. Jim had just finished screwing a stud in place and began to lower the scaffold while Steve cut the next stud at the workbench. When Jim reached the ground, Steve started to drag the new stud to him. When Steve was about five feet away, Jim was suddenly jerked off the scaffold, lifted about three feet into the air, and thrown back down, landing shoulder first. He lay there shaking, then stopped moving, apparently unconscious. A moment later he screamed, "Shit! I've been electrocuted!" A few minutes later, Jim sat up, moving his arms. He swung his head back, acting as if he was trying to rouse himself from a deep sleep. He got up and started to walk, faltering a bit at first. But within a minute he was standing and bending his legs. By this time, nearly everyone at the work site had gathered around. To their relief, he seemed unhurt. Through the rest of the day, workers drifted by again to check and make sure that Jim was all right.

The predominantly female workers at the apparel plant also organized life-cycle celebrations, most frequently for birthdays and baby showers. Management does not support the celebrations, so the women squeeze them into their lunch period, usually with a cake and small presents. When a worker is hospitalized, not only does everyone sign a card, but many visit the hospital after work. All of these practices brought workers together in ways that could and frequently did overcome ethnic and newcomer-American differences. In the apparel plant, however, race still persisted as a fundamental partition. As one Haitian immigrant worker explained:

They all went outside. But the other group of people went inside. They went inside. Then, some outside. Then, me, if they invite me to something, I go. But if they don't invite me, I don't go. My car was parked nearby. I got into the car. I was eating my lunch. I saw groups of Cubans together. I see them in the backyard. But no one told me whether I had to give money or to help in anyway. They did not tell me anything. I did not know anything about it. It was the first time that I saw them partying.

On a day-to-day basis, segregation by race and national origin predominates over solidarity. Segregation is most obvious at lunch, when at every work site each person eats with someone of their own group and talks with only those of their own group. At the airport hotel, there were separate Latino, Haitian, and black seating areas. The few white Americans joined the American blacks and spoke in English. Haitian immigrants spoke exclusively in Creole, and the Latinos exclusively in Spanish. At the luxury hotel, workers established the same ethnic segregation, although with more "floaters," workers who crossed groups. There, the few American blacks either sat alone or floated, often sitting with newcomer whites or Latinos during lunch. Similarly, some Haitian immigrants who spoke English and Spanish ventured outside their ethnic group.

The apparel plant enforced lunchtime segregation most strongly, yet informally. On one occasion, a Haitian immigrant woman, apparently mistakenly, assumed one of these reserved Miami Cuban seats. A Miami Cuban woman politely asked the Haitian immigrant woman to leave, explaining that this was her customary seat. The Haitian immigrant woman assented, but a Haitian immigrant woman who was looking on objected somewhat quietly. The following day, however, the woman who had objected forced the issue by assuming the Miami Cuban's seat. When the Miami Cuban again requested her seat, not quite as politely this time, the Miami Haitian woman responded that it was a free country and there were no reserved seats in the cafeteria. As the argument progressed, she added that this was just another example of discrimination against blacks in general and Haitians in particular. The argument escalated into a shouting match, with interested onlookers sometimes adding their own opinions. It did not stop until one of the managers intervened.

The unionized construction industry maintains segregation through occupational allocation of the separate construction trades: unskilled laborers are primarily American blacks; skilled trades such as electricians and plumbers remain overwhelmingly American white; and carpenters contain a mix of American whites and newcomer Latinos. Each trade has its own task, which is done either separately in large sites or in sequence, so that members of different trades interact only minimally. Given that the trades are largely segregated by ethnicity, little interaction occurs across ethnic groups.

Interethnic and newcomer-American interaction most commonly appears in a joking relationship. A white American carpenter may say to his Miami Cuban coworker or to an African American laborer, "Hey buddy, stop hanging around and get back to work. This ain't break time." The recipient of this "joke" usually smiles and goes on his way. Occasionally, the joking expression releases unconscious prejudice, but in a way that avoids open aggression. A white American coworker claimed you had to watch out for Miami Cuban insulators. "They carry big fucking knives and they'll use them." A Miami Cuban insulator overheard the comment but did not act.[3]

BECOMING AN AMERICAN WORKER

For the overwhelming majority of American immigrants, becoming American includes becoming an American worker. Not all American workers are alike, however. For many Miami Cuban and other newcomer construction workers, becoming an American worker means working within the American labor movement, where they learn that workers do not have to accept unfair or dangerous working conditions, that they can legitimately stand up to their bosses. As one Miami Cuban carpenter is fond of saying, "I came here for [being] anti-communist, not for [being a] *come mierda* [asshole]. I don't have to take everything they feed me. I, too, have ideas that work, and all I ask is for a chance to show you."

The primarily Latino workers in the apparel plant also wanted to show that they knew a better way, that the bureaucratized, depersonalized American ways of their new owners and managers were not appropriate. They, too, got away with their resistance, at least in the short run. They defeated the American plant owners' rigid hierarchy and rules, but the American owner-managers gave up and sold the plant rather than adapting to the newcomers. The American company did not sell the plant solely because their newcomer Latino workforce subtly resisted them. Global competition from low-cost labor offshore has assaulted the apparel industry nationwide. Perhaps the plant would have closed even if the workers had bought into the new American management style. But at least through the 1980s, Miami's apparel industry struggled more successfully than most of the rest of the industry in the United States. The availability of hardworking, relatively inexpensive newcomer immigrant labor had attracted the American owners from Chicago in the first place. They just did not realize how important culture could be.

In the hotels and restaurants, the culture of the workers was less important. Workers were not culturally homogeneous and, most importantly, they had no solidarity to forge a broad resistance. They had neither the organized working tradition of the unionized construction workers nor the relatively homogeneous culture and previously comparatively positive experiences of the apparel workers. Hotel and restaurant workers were alienated from management and from each other. Their work was compartmentalized, competitive, and frequently conflictual.

To be an American worker also entails conflict in the workplace. In Miami, conflict is almost always interpreted as newcomer-American or more generally ethnic. When Jean grabbed a bundle of material from

Angelina, Jean and Angelina—along with just about all the other workers in the plant—interpreted this as a Haitian immigrant trying to get back at a Miami Cuban. While workers interpreted virtually all workplace conflict as ethnic, in reality nearly all workplace conflict had its roots in the nature of the work. The apparel plant production process was based upon the piece rate, and thus encouraged workers to compete. Conflict in the restaurants erupted under the pressure of getting food quickly to customers.

Unionized construction workers frequently viewed conflict as class-based: that they, for example, did the work of building a fancy hotel for others to enjoy. A young Miami Cuban American carpenter, for example, asserted, "Yeah, there's always going to be prejudice, but it's not that bad here. Everyone's in the same boat. Everyone gets sweaty, dirty, and smelly." Similarly, as one American white carpenter stated about his Miami Cuban coworker, "I've known that son of a bitch for years, we're brothers in wood." Jack, another American white, stated, "I know a lot of Cubans." Pointing to David, an older Miami Cuban, Jack added, "I've worked with him for years. We borrow each other's shit all the time."

The construction workers' alienation from management even extended to a distrust of their own union management, who they felt were more interested in protecting union management perks than in serving the workers. Nevertheless, the union did provide them with a solidarity that hotel and restaurant workers lacked. In contrast, the apparel plant union played little role. The paternalistic, more Latino management style of the previous owner, ironically a white American, fit them well. They expressed dissatisfaction with the new owners' American management style by subtly resisting pressures to increase production and not through union-organized resistance.

Race emerged as a key factor in determining workers' reactions to management and their interactions with each other. Black construction workers had the worst jobs. Black hotel and restaurant workers were placed in the "back of the house." Haitian immigrants fared even worse than American blacks, taking abuse not only from Americans, but also from newcomer Latinos. As in the business community and the schools, becoming American in the workplace entails learning and adopting American racial stereotypes, making and enforcing firm distinctions between black and whites.

Yet on a day-to-day basis, conflict and racism do not overwhelm the workplace. People do need to get their jobs done, and usually this entails some form of cooperation. It is just as American to pull together to get something done as it is to expect to have to overcome differences of culture, class, ethnicity, and race to get it done. Workers also pulled together in response to workplace accidents. Women workers organized celebrations of birthdays, along with showers for weddings and babies. For those moments, workers came together positively.

The dominant American value that permitted jobs to get done was routinization of production. Implicit rules of cooperation governed most daily work. Frequently this included ethnic segregation, staying away from those perceived to be different. Nevertheless, ultimately for all the workers, becoming American meant daily interaction with non-Americans. Sometimes these other newcomers were subordinates, other times they were peers and frequently they exercised some degree of power.

Becoming American is often a power struggle. Differences of ethnicity or status often become emotionally-charged emblems of deeper struggles rooted in the workplace. The same ethnic solidarity that catapulted newcomer Cubans into political office and entrepreneurial success was also expressed by Pepe, the Miami Cuban craftsman who reached a position of authority in a union and proceeded to open the doors to other newcomer Latinos, thereby having to become adept at navigating the political waters of the American labor movement. Similarly, newcomer Latina apparel workers struggled with their new American owner-managers over how to organize the workplace. They also vied with each other over the seemingly more mundane issue of getting the best bundles to sew, just as hotel and restaurant workers struggled with overcoming their workplace tedium and maintaining individual autonomy. These struggles were all rooted in the nature of the work. They occur wherever there are construction, apparel, and hotel and restaurant workers. But in Miami, they were interpreted as ethnic, newcomer-American, and linguistic battles.

FOUR

Just Comes and Cover-Ups

African Americans and Haitians in High School

"Everybody's the same in every way. Everybody is equal. You black, I'm black, right? You know there shouldn't be no discrimination between nobody at this school."

—A fourteen-year-old African American high school girl

A fifteen-year-old Miami Haitian boy added to the class discussion, "You should tell them we are African 'cause all-a-us came on the slave ships from Africa. Some got off here and some got off there. We're all African." The class spontaneously erupted into applause. An African American girl hedged, "To me being an American is believing in the country that you're in right now *and* believing in your heritage." Another African American girl appended a bit more distance between African Americans and her Miami Haitian classmates: "These people want to come over here and stuff and they want all the privileges and stuff but why they don't want to be called Americans?" Another African American girl agreed, "I can understand people coming over here from other countries. I just don't understand why they don't want to be American. They have their privileges. What's the country gonna be called? You have a million different nationalities. Russia is called Russia. They are Russian people. Jamaica is called Jamaica. Hey, if you don't want to be called American, get out!"

This classroom discussion encapsulates this book's primary themes—diversity, context, and power. The debate over the difference between being black and being Haitian is fundamentally different from the interactions either in the business community or at the work sites. Not all immigrants have the same opportunities for assimilation available to them. Being a black immigrant profoundly affects the nature of relations and the available assimilation paths. Within the context of black, inner-city schools, Haitian immigrants either remain Haitians or they become black Americans. Within this limited context, African American youth have cultural power. Haitian immigrants in these schools assimilate, at least superficially, to inner-city African American youth culture.

This chapter examines the interaction between black Haitian immigrant adolescents and African American adolescents in a Miami inner-city high school. The school sits on the informal boundary between Little Haiti and Liberty City, the largest concentration of African Americans in the greater Miami area. Haitian immigrants began entering the school in the early 1980s. When we began our research in the late 1980s, the school was about half Haitian and half African American. By the mid-1990s, it was estimated to have 80 to 90 percent Haitian students. Precise numbers are unavailable because the school district only asks country of origin for foreign-born students. For the native-born, students are categorized only as Hispanic, black, Asian, non-Hispanic white, or other. Thus, second-generation Haitians appear in school statistics simply as black. Both the school system and many of their African American peers insist that they have no choice but to assimilate to America's racial system.

PREJUDICE AND ASSIMILATION

During the 1970s and 1980s, no other immigrant group suffered more prejudice and discrimination than Haitians. Cases abound: there has been the U.S. Coast Guard attempting to intercept boats of Haitians before they left Haitian waters, the disproportionate incarceration of undocumented Haitians who made it to U.S. shores, and the highest disapproval rating of any national group for political asylum requests. Repeatedly, local South Florida and national officials have identified Haitians as a health threat. In the late 1970s, tuberculosis was allegedly endemic among Haitians; in the early 1980s, the Center for Disease Control identified Haitians as one of the primary groups at risk for AIDS, along with homosexuals, hemophiliacs, and intravenous drug abusers. In spite of the removal of Haitians from that list, the Food and Drug Administration in the late 1980s officially refused to accept blood donations from individuals of Haitian descent (Stepick 1998).

Negative stereotyping of Haitians is hardly new or peculiar to Haitian refugees (McCormick 1996). The anthropologist Sidney Mintz remarked, "Few countries in modern times have received as bad press at the hands of foreign observers as Haiti" (Mintz 1974). The medical doctor and anthropologist Paul Farmer maintains, "At worst, journalistic writing about Haiti distorts events and processes in predictable ways, helping to perpetuate a series of particularly potent myths about Haiti and Haitians" (Farmer 1994). Robert Lawless devoted an entire book to the subject, *Haiti's Bad Press*, in which he writes, "Few people would disagree with the statement that favorable reports about Haiti are as rare as positive declarations on the nutritional value of cannibalism or the healing power of black magic" (Lawless 1992).

These prejudices mark the experiences of Haitians in the United States. Rosina, born in the Bahamas of Haitian parents, asserts, "It's one thing I don't like about American people, they're always pickin' on Haitians. Like, any time, like, two Americans get into, like, an argument or somethin' like, I mean the curse word they use is 'Haitian' . . . it's some type of curse word." Guerda, who stated that Haitian slurs upset her, claimed an African American had just accused a Miami Haitian of eating cat for lunch. "I mean, I'm proud of my country [Haiti] and I will never deny it."

In the early 1980s, when Haitian immigrants first started entering the high school where we did our research, conflict episodically convulsed the school, forcing administrators to close it temporarily a number of times. Students severely ridiculed and beat up anyone who looked Haitian or spoke Creole or accented English. African American students mocked newly arrived Haitian boys for playing soccer instead of football and basketball, a greater sin to many African American students than not wearing deodorant or "dressing funny." My experience as a fieldworker revealed that the negative cultural stereotypes of Haitians being dirty and smelly (a stereotype that is frequently applied to all blacks or to all poor people) was quite the opposite of actual Haitian hygiene. Haitian culture places a strong emphasis on cleanliness.

Real cultural differences nevertheless did exist. The Miami Haitian boys refused to touch a football, complaining that it was too little. The teachers compromised by permitting the Haitian immigrants to throw a soccer ball around as if it were a football. Through the mid-1980s, most of the newly immigrated Haitian girls would not wear the gym uniform of red shorts and a white T-shirt. Many failed physical education before the teachers figured out that Haitian immigrant parents would not let their daughters wear shorts, and the girls were afraid to disobey their parents, even if it meant getting F's. The teachers again compromised, allowing the girls to wear long culottes that resembled skirts.

A waitress at the McDonald's a block from the high school asserted that the African American students treat Miami Haitians "like dogs," especially their fellow students. African Americans tried to abuse her as well. Thinking that she was Haitian, they would demand, "Hurry up, you dumb Haitian!" She set them straight right away. She is Bahamian. Several times she had crossed over to the customer side of the counter to defend Miami Haitian students who seemed reluctant to fight back.

She maintained that much of this attitude comes from Americans' terrible image of Haiti. Their image of the Bahamas as a vacation paradise, fortunately for her, is entirely different.

Through the 1980s, the high school's administrators and staff with few exceptions struggled sincerely and vigorously to serve the newly arrived Haitians, but they did not have the readily available resources or knowledge with which to serve them. The principal and the school district had no previous experience with Haitian immigrants. They did not have ready access to New York and other areas of the northeastern United States that had years of experience in the schools and had produced numerous Haitian immigrant professionals who could have been recruited to Miami. They did not have pools of certified ESL instructors familiar with Haitian Creole, as already existed for Spanish, since Cubans began arriving in Miami twenty years before Haitians did.

In spite of the best intentions, occasionally teachers and administrators reinforced the negative stereotypes of Haitians by the ways they treated them. For example, in January 1986, about thirty-five newly arrived Haitian students required a separate classroom, but the administration had already assigned all existing space in the extremely overcrowded school. The only available space was a partially enclosed outdoor area designed for equipment storage. One wall was a roll-up section of chain link bars. The new arrivals remained in this space all day every day. As word of this room spread through the school, it acquired a nickname, "Krome North," a reference to the Immigration and Naturalization Service detention center in the Everglades on the farthest edge of Miami.

Yet prejudice against Haitian immigrants was far more blatant outside the school. During the 1986 soccer quarterfinals, the high school played a prestigious private high school. The team consisted solely of Haitian immigrant students. Throughout the game, the players and coaches from the private school taunted the players by ridiculing their accents and skin color. A year later, the same thing happened when the high school played a public school with a mixed Cuban American and white American student body. When rain began to fall, some of the Haitian immigrant parents in the stands made makeshift umbrellas from sticks and fronds. The Latinos on the other side went wild and jeered rudely, shouting racial slurs and mockingly pretending to be gorillas.

In an early 1990s survey of Miami Haitian eighth- and ninth-graders in South Florida schools, over 60 percent claimed that they had experienced anti-Haitian discrimination in the United States. Those who were born in the United States reported even more discrimination that those Haitians who were born abroad (Fernandez-Kelly 1994; Portes and MacLeod 1996).

We asked: "Do the football players mix, black Americans and Haitians, during and after school? Are they really one big, happy family?" An African American star of the football team replied, "Oh yeah, definitely, There's Beaujelleaux. He's Haitian and he walks home from school with James Lemarre."

Another day, a Miami Haitian student remarked that James Lemarre's mother visited her mother frequently and the two would speak in Haitian Creole because James's mother spoke no English. The next day, a girl who had heard this confronted James in school, first speaking to him in Creole and then declaring in English, "Now don't pretend that you don't know what I'm saying! I know your mother and she doesn't even speak English!"

In the parlance of the high school Miami Haitians, James Lemarre was being a "cover-up" or "undercover," hiding his Haitian roots by passing as an African American. Some claim to be Jamaican or Bahamian, but if a student has the right dress, the right talk, and the right moves, he or she apparently has assimilated to being African American. Male Miami Haitian cover-ups, like African American boys, base their dress style on one central theme: athletics. A male minimally sports spotlessly clean, expensive leather high-top sneakers, $65.00 BKs (British Knights), Nikes, or Adidas. One *never* wears dirty sneakers to school. As one African American senior reported, "Only teachers and Haitians do that." In the late 1980s and early 1990s, styles included closely cropped heads with incised designs, often spelling out Nike or Adidas. They wore baggy shirts in muted colors, Bugle Boy jeans with a neat pleat, and not infrequently several gold chains, perhaps a necklace with a large wooden pendant shaped like the continent of Africa, a fancy looking watch, and for some, a beeper. By the late 1990s, styles had changed slightly, but undoubtedly they were still the styles of African American inner-city youth.

Undercover Miami Haitian girls passing as African Americans dress with considerably more freedom of style, more sexually suggestive than the *just come* Haitians, that is, those Haitians who are still identifiable as being from Haiti. They and African American girls are much more conscious of color, coordinating their clothes. They wear short skirts and sport fancy "do's," or hairstyles. In physical education, they wear the most revealing, tiniest short shorts and tight T-shirts.

One has to not only look African American, one has to sound like an African American, although preferably, as one Miami Haitian girl put it, "without the cuss words." Undercovers, like their African American peers, cock their heads to the side and utter things like "Mah maaan," "fresh," and "Don't dis me, man" (which could mean anything from don't ignore me to don't lie to me). Saturated with idioms from rap music, the language is decidedly black English. Sentences have a subject and a gerund, but no connecting verb: "They fightin' " or "She comin'." The word "ain't" begins many questions. "Ain't she comin', man?" In addition, the verb form of choice is "be," as in, "They be here."

The moves are equally necessary. Hubert, a Miami Haitian, visits the teacher's desk with Hank, an African American. As he returns to his seat, Hubert struts. He chats with a Miami Haitian girl in the corner. During the brief conversation, he periodically and distinctly scratches and squeezes his testicles. In answer to someone asking for help with their work, he declares, "No pain, no gain." The moves and interactions are standardized, appearing almost rehearsed. Miami Haitian cover-ups perform them so well that it becomes frequently impossible to distinguish Haitian-born from African American students. James Lemarre was an exceptionally successful cover-up. He spoke with no accent and never indicated his true ethnicity. He let the whole school assume that he was American-born. His football teammates presumed he was African American. No teacher guessed that he was Haitian. Even other Miami Haitians were surprised to learn of his Haitian roots.

The combined prejudices from the broader American society and those specifically within the high school urge Miami Haitian adolescents to assimilate rapidly and to simultaneously engage in ethnic suicide, to cover up their Haitian origins. To these Miami Haitians, as described by Yves Labissiere (1995), "American" means specifically African American, and even more precisely, inner-city, poor African Americans.

One cannot miss those Miami Haitians who have not yet assimilated to African American culture. In the morning and during lunch, "just comes" pack "Haitian Hall," where they speak Creole exclusively. The guys wear dress pants, cotton button-down shirts, and loafers of soft leather with no socks. Like Esther and Irlande, many girls wear long skirts or dresses that cover much of their bodies. They seemingly have no idea of what is considered fashionable dress in the United States. They are also very shy and almost never speak to anyone except the teacher. Everyone knows these girls are Haitian immigrants even before they speak.

In the classrooms, the process of assimilation is enacted daily. Toward the front of an ESL classroom sit a few boys speaking Creole among themselves. One of them, Max, wears slacks, an ironed shirt, and loafers. He assuredly is not cool, but he is very anxious to learn and stays after class to complete his assignments, even though he will be late for lunch. Meanwhile, Telfort and Arrive hang out in the back of the classroom with a group of four or five boys who are obviously rebellious and uninterested in school. Telfort and Arrive are the most verbal and uncooperative. Arrive rarely speaks English and refuses to do most of the assignments. Telfort got into a fistfight the first day with Aarold, who dresses and acts like some of the African American boys. By the third month of school, Aarold began to show an obstinate side that he did not have in the beginning of the year, and he sometimes comes late to class without an admit. Arrive, Telfort, Aarold, and their friends are in the process of transforming their positive academic orientation into an adversarial attitude toward school.

Miami Haitians with enough resources to live in the middle-class African American or ethnically mixed suburbs encounter a more prosperous and optimistic America. They interact with more adolescent peers who believe that education promises a better future. They are also less likely to encounter intense, specifically anti-Haitian prejudice and more likely to encounter general anti-black racism. They live in an environment that more readily permits positive expressions of their Haitian culture. Middle-class Miami Haitians are more likely to retain pride in their national origins and become hyphenated Haitian-Americans.

In contrast, those Miami Haitian adolescents who are residents of the inner city and attend a school with over 90 percent black students encounter a different America, an overwhelmingly poor black America. Their proximal hosts, that is, the group into which mainstream America categorizes the immigrants, are African Americans (Mittleberg and Waters 1992). The people they see daily in their neighborhood are neither white nor middle class. When these Haitian immigrants assimilate, when they Americanize, they become not generic, mainstream Americans but specifically African Americans and primarily the poor African Americans most vulnerable to American racism. They assimilate rapidly to African American body language, speech patterns, sports, dress, and hairstyles. They adopt the culture of those immediately around them, the inner-city culture of primarily poor African American youth that is both romanticized and demeaned by mainstream America. Mainstream America celebrates and commercializes inner-city African American music and styles, but it also negatively stereotypes inner-city youth as violent and opposed to values concerning work, education, and family.

Within this context of prejudice, African Americans are concerned with affirming and justifying their identity as discriminated against by American citizens. One African American girl maintained,

> You can't blame the black people for feeling that way (that foreigners are taking their jobs) because we have been here for years and we have been at the bottom of the totem pole and we still haven't made it to the top or the middle of the totem pole and you have people comin' over here, Haitians and Cubans and we as black Americans are not afraid to work. Back in the fifties, we were the most hard-working people. I don't think anybody else in this world, in this nation, have worked harder than the black people. We have been through wars. We have been through struggles and marched down streets, were beat, killed, spat-on, raped, you name it, but we made it through, regardless whether we are together now. In parts of the US, we are still put down, basically, but it's not like in Africa. They have been saying that the Haitians are doin' this and that, and that the American blacks are lazy. That's not true!

Many African American students maintained that they had to work or try harder because they are black. One Miami Haitian boy said that the only way that any black person could be free in America was if there were two countries: one for blacks and one for whites.

In spite of a keen awareness of racism, African American students positively evaluate being an American. Over 80 percent of those surveyed in the high school where we conducted research in the late 1980s asserted that they are "strongly" proud to be American and not a single one indicated a lack of pride in being American. In a class discussion, one African American boy declared, "To be an American is opportunity, to come here to get jobs, to say what you want to say, to be able to say 'damn' on the street like you might not in Russia. Being an American is the life, believe me. I won't change it for anything. If I go somewhere else, I'm still an American. I won't change it for anybody, believe *that!*"

The frustration of confronting racism produces resentment towards blacks who abandon their heritage. One class discussed an African

American girl who was a star debater. One student referred to her as a "black-white" girl, someone who probably grew up in an upper-middle-class neighborhood around lots of whites, had a good education, and learned to speak like a white girl. Another girl added that a "black-white girl" could be a dark-skinned girl from a broken family who was sent to a white environment or to a white school to be raised and influenced by white people. An African American boy declared, "A lot of you don't realize, there are black people out there that are whiter than Mr. Schlegel [the teacher]. There are black people out there that wants to be white, you know what I'm sayin'? You'll find a lot of black women, they're fair like my complexion and they'll say 'I'm white' and I have come in contact with them and I tell them I am black and proud of it."

One African American boy claimed that he thought blacks hurt themselves more than other people hurt them. "We were in slavery for centuries, but we still will not help each other. We only worry about ourselves, whereas other people will try to help each other get ahead. I think this is from training in years of being suppressed. That when they [blacks] get a chance to be on top, they don't worry about anybody else, they only worry about themselves."

In short, for most African American high-school students, the realities of racism and discrimination compel a unity based on race. Those who ignore this solidarity by denying their black identity are akin to a selfish individual abandoning his family. Correspondingly, Miami Haitians who express their cultural identity by speaking Creole or accented English instead of black English, by playing soccer instead of football, by dressing differently, these Miami Haitians also challenge African Americans' sense of communal solidarity among all black people. Moreover, the extraordinary specifically anti-Haitian prejudice in South Florida encourages many Miami Haitians to abandon their national heritage.

As Miami Haitian teenagers Americanize by adopting particular aspects of African American inner-city adolescent culture—and while African Americans apparently do not adopt anything that is Haitian—

they reflect a classic assimilation process. In general, young immigrants or the children of immigrants assimilate rapidly. Miami Haitians differ from the assimilation of most other immigrants only in the particular subculture of America into which they assimilate. Yet, as the chapter introduction indicates, this assimilation entails conflict based in American racism. While African American peers insist that Miami Haitians identify as black, others advise that Miami Haitians should maintain a cultural distance from African Americans. A Latino teacher discouraged his students from picking up any American slang that sounded like it came from the ghetto. He told his students that when they apply for a job and use black English, they are automatically looked upon as being ignorant.

A white American teacher reluctantly admitted that white teachers often make the assumption that all blacks are stupid. Numerous teachers, including a few African Americans, held African American students responsible for inadequate discipline in their classrooms. As a Miami Haitian teacher asserted, "This kind of behavior would never be tolerated in Haiti."

The conflicting pressures create a tortured self-identity for Miami Haitian adolescents. In a class with mostly Haitian immigrant students, one Miami Haitian asked, "Why can't we [the Haitians] be ourselves?" Other Miami Haitians joined in. One girl said that any time an American says, "'You Haitian!' it means, 'You are stupid, smelly, and dirty!'" Another girl asserted that the worst thing a Miami Haitian could do was to deny his or her true cultural identity, to go undercover. A formerly undercover Miami Haitian wearing army fatigues and combat boots asked, "How does a Haitian dress?" "Like this!" quickly responds a Miami Haitian boy, proudly displaying his expensive-looking dress pants with pleats in the front, a Polo brand shirt, leather loafers, and no socks. A Miami Haitian on the other side of the room, who dresses like an American jock, says, "Assimilate . . . the sooner the better!" Another Miami Haitian retorts, "No. . . . be yourself because people put you down for pretending to be something else." In spite of his reply, this Miami Haitian dresses like an American, with stone-washed jeans and leather high-tops, speaks English well, and knows a lot of slang. The self he presents to peers has become an African American self.

In a 1989 survey of Miami Haitian students, over 70 percent maintained that they had no desire to become American citizens. When asked how they regarded being and becoming American, Miami Haitian students responded: "Don't give a shit. Dirty. Rude. Less class. Black Americans are disrespectful of their peers and grownups. They don't wash enough. I am an American citizen by birth, not choice. Too much crime, fighting and killing, especially among children. My mother automatically stereotypes black Americans as thieves."

In a class with primarily Miami Haitian students, students debated the merits of living in the United States versus Haiti. A girl who arrived in 1986 spoke first: "I don't like it here." Another girl added that she had been back to Haiti for visits and she wished she could live there. A boy who had adopted the appearance of being an African American declared, "I don't like it here just like everyone else." Two other boys revealed ambivalence, indicating they had not yet made up their minds, while another stated that he liked it here but wanted to live in his own country.

Going undercover, becoming a cover-up, is perhaps the most common way to address this ambivalence. In the spring of 1989, the school newspaper wrote an article on one of the first Miami Haitian girls to become a cheerleader. For two years before this article appeared, the girl had kept her Haitian background secret. Another Miami Haitian girl had kept her heritage a secret while she dated a popular African American boy. She arrived at school one day to find her name and the word "undercover" scrawled across the front steps of the school.

Phede came from Haiti to the United States when he was twelve years old. He quickly assimilated. He became a cover-up, hiding his Haitian identity by Americanizing his name to Fred. He spoke English without an accent and never spoke Creole, even at home. He worked at McDonalds full-time, sang in the church choir, and became an honor student in high school. He wanted to be a lawyer someday. He had a good-looking steady girlfriend, an African American. One day she came to visit with Fred, to talk to him while he took his break at McDonalds. While they were talking, Fred's sister arrived. She addressed Fred in Haitian Creole. She blew his cover, and he blew his cool. Fred screamed at her to never, ever speak Creole to him again. He did not want to be known as Haitian. Four days later, he bought a .22 caliber revolver for $50, drove to an empty lot near his home and killed himself with a bullet to his chest.

Through the 1980s, Miami Haitian adolescents struggled with the conflicting pulls of maintaining their parents' pride in Haiti and confronting anti-Haitian prejudice from others. Many went undercover at school, yet still evinced the typical immigrant respect for education. While language barriers prevented many from doing well academically, the majority of Miami Haitian youth tried to succeed in school, and a significant number graduated at the top of the class and went on to ivy league colleges. In the 1990s, a new alternative emerged when some Miami Haitians began to express an African American identity at the same time as they maintained pride in their Haitian origins.

POWER AND PUBLIC PRIDE

A Miami Haitian boy who has been in this country all his life defended the undercovers by advancing the view that "just because a person wants to become an American, you know, doesn't mean they have to forget their heritage and everything. When people wonder why are all these people are crossing the border they are forgetting that their ancestors come from England and Scotland. When they ask me where I'm from, I say from Haiti, straight up."

Through the 1980s, Miami Haitians were disparaged, and they responded by assimilating as rapidly as possible. As they became accepted by their American peers, some were able to maintain or, for those who had become cover-ups, rediscover pride in their Haitian origins. During the football season, for example, the school had regular pep rallies before the games. The whole school piled into the auditorium and there were songs and cheers and general, orchestrated chaos. In the mid-1980s, when a group of Miami Haitians performed a Haitian dance on stage, they were booed off the stage. But by the early 1990s, these rallies had taken on a distinctly Haitian flavor. Students applauded traditional Haitian dances. They came to accept a new tradition at an event that had been narrowly, even ethnocentrically American.

American sports became a vehicle for Miami Haitians to gain acceptance. In 1989, five Miami Haitians started on the football team, and two of these were star players. There were also Miami Haitian starters on the varsity basketball team. The basketball coach claimed that the members of his team were blind to ethnicity. The team was a tight, unified one. The players not only ate together, but they also associated in many other activities. According to the coach, "Five years ago, few Haitians tried out for the team or even knew how to play the game. Now they are coming out in large numbers, and these are boys who have assimilated and who feel confident in an area that is typically American."

Outside of sports, the emergence of pride in Haitian culture was even more evident. In the spring most of the junior class prepared to take a statewide standardized achievement test, the PSAT. It had become customary for several students to go around to classes doing a rap song about the PSAT. The lyrics were original and were accompanied by music from a boom box. When the teacher came into one of the junior classes one day in mid-March 1989, she heard the PSAT rap being done in Creole by a group of new arrivals. After school and on weekends, the just-come Miami Haitians had gotten together and translated the English lyrics into Creole. The rhythms of Creole fit perfectly, and the class of primarily Miami Haitian students got such a kick out of it that the teachers opened the sliding partition that separated the room from two other classes that had mainly African American students. The new arrivals performed it for them, too. The African Americans loudly cheered the performance, and the Miami Haitian PSAT rap was added to the black English tour of classrooms.

The advanced journalism class, which published the school newspaper, also embraced positive interaction between African Americans and Miami Haitians. All of the students socialized daily with each other across ethnic boundaries and sat together with no evidence of ethnic divisiveness. On the last day of school before Christmas break in 1988, the class had a party, and the students were discussing what type of food to bring for the event. The teacher asked for a certain dish that was popular in Haiti. There were two Miami Haitian girls in the class at the time. One of the girls, who appeared to be a more recent arrival, said that she never ate Haitian food and that her mother didn't cook any. The other girl, who appeared to be more Americanized, retorted that she knew the dish well and volunteered to bring some in. She then announced to the other girl, "I'm a real Haitian, girl!"

This ostensibly more Americanized student who reasserted pride in her heritage is not alone. In the late 1980s and through the 1990s, there emerged an increasingly large group of Miami Haitian students who insisted upon speaking Creole, even in the presence of African Americans. They wore traditional Haitian dress styles to school and pressed for more activities in the school that would reflect their interests and culture. By the mid-1990s, greater numbers of Miami Haitians maintained both their Haitian heritage and a positive view of African Americans. In 1996, one Miami Haitian ninth grader asserted, "We are all black. We should all get together." Another maintained, "The white people judge all the blacks in the U.S. the same, no matter where you came from." And another added, "You should judge people by the way they are, not by the way they look."

Two factors, one structural and another individual, enabled positive transformation of relationships and attitudes. First, the demographics of the student population had given Miami Haitians an overwhelming majority within the school. By the mid-1990s, African Americans were estimated to be less than 20 percent and maybe as little as 10 percent of the student body. Those who slandered and denigrated Miami Haitians had lost the protection of being in the majority. They no longer had the power of numbers to enforce their denigrating misrepresentations of

Haitians. In the early 1980s, Miami Haitians constituted a small minority of the student body. When insulted, they had little recourse in the face of overwhelming numbers. Within the school's circumscribed environment of student relationships, African American students dominated. They could demean Miami Haitians as unworthy newcomers, lower than the lowest of American society. Miami Haitians could not readily retort. While Haitian newcomers may have had pride in their Haitian origins, they had no mechanism for convincing their African American peers that Haitians deserved respect. Most of student culture simply devalued what Miami Haitians valued and accomplished. Speaking more than one language (Haitian Creole and French) was inconsequential if one could not speak English. Being well dressed in French styles was being a sissy or too fancy for an American high school. Being respectful and passive toward teachers was inappropriate for the majority culture. As a minority, Miami Haitians could not combat these negative interpretations of their culture.

For most immigrant groups, at least some of these cultural traits, such as respect for teachers and learning, are rewarded by larger institutions, particularly teachers and family. But for Haitians, the broad anti-Haitian prejudice in South Florida diluted teachers' appreciation of Haitian students. While some recognized positive traits among Haitians and rewarded them, others occasionally uttered anti-Haitian remarks or balanced their positive evaluation of Miami Haitian students with critical comments.

Haitian immigrant parents could not adequately support Haitian values either. Not only did they confront pervasive prejudice, but the vagaries of immigration often split families, with one and sometimes both parents remaining in Haiti while the children were in Miami. Single parents and relatives had difficulty reinforcing values and discipline. In Haiti, not only were both parents usually available, but so were an extended family of grandparents, uncles, and aunts, who could punish misbehaving children. The generally anti-Haitian immigration policy of the United States made it less likely that these relatives would be present in the United States.

These forces combined in the 1980s to convince many Miami Haitian students to abandon their heritage, that to survive as adolescents and to get along with their African American peers they had to cover up, to assimilate "the sooner the better." The immediate power of African American students within the school, reinforced by the broader American society and complemented by the diminished power of Miami Haitian families, compelled the submission of Miami Haitian students.

While African American students had the power within the context of the school to oblige Miami Haitians to assimilate, outside of the school African Americans remained a disempowered minority. Haitian immigrant adults in the workplace, for example, made no effort to assimilate to African American culture. Because of the power of Miami Cubans in Miami, Miami Haitian adults were more likely to learn Spanish than African American English. Even within the school, teachers and administrators urged Haitian immigrants to Americanize into mainstream American culture, to speak standard rather than black English. Thus, in the broader Miami context beyond the school, African Americans did not dominate Miami Haitians or anyone else. Only within the narrow confines of student culture, where they constituted a majority, did African American inner city youth culture exercise power. As Miami Haitian student numbers increased, African American power to affect Miami Haitians diminished.

Secondly, the achievements of individual Miami Haitian students underlay their reassertion of Haitian culture and the concomitant positive evaluation by their African American peers. The students who forcefully, self-consciously promoted Haitian culture were those who had been most successful in high school, the ones who were in the advanced classes or who had achieved success in sports. They were both African American *and* Haitian. They could not be "dissed"—ridiculed or subjected to disrespect—for not being like African Americans.

In contrast, in the basic classes, where students had not evidenced academic or extracurricular accomplishments, students were more likely to present problems for teachers. They were more likely to exhibit the negative attitude toward education attributed to inner-city, poor African Americans. One teacher claimed there were few problems in her upper-level classes. "However," she added, "problems occur when the class consists predominantly of Haitian females who have been here long enough to speak the language without an accent, especially if they are limited in academic potential or interest. Nothing seems to help in that situation."

In the 1990s, Miami police apprehended increasing numbers of Miami Haitian youth, and Miami Haitian gangs emerged. In the 1980s, Miami Haitian community leaders deemed jobs and a secure immigration status as the most important needs in the Miami Haitian community. In the 1990s, the same leaders identified their concerns over the future of Miami's Haitian youth as the number one community priority (Stepick and Stepick 1994). Miami Haitian youth increasingly divided themselves into two types: those who maintained aspects of their culture while still assimilating and those who rejected their roots and assimilated fully to a minority, inner-city, poor African American youth culture.

Individual teachers could promote tolerance and acceptance. An innovative and popular English teacher, an African American, tried to teach her students to survive in an ethnically diverse community without abandoning their heritage. She moved excitedly about the room with a sophisticated flourish and imitated a southern drawl. She touched a girl on the shoulder affectionately, calling her "child." Suddenly she switched dialects and became a *señorita*, rolling her *r*'s deliciously, enunciating a perfect Mexican accent. She then switched to black English. Throughout she held the students spellbound. She taught them that she could talk street jive and be proud of it, but that proper English must be used when the occasion calls for it, when confronting the larger, white-dominated society. She entertainingly and effectively communicated the beauty and wealth of multiculturalism. When a student asked her if he had to do a homework assignment, she replied, "You don't have to do anything except stay black and die." The class, including the inquisitive student, exploded in laughter.

Human tragedy also galvanizes different ethnic groups. In the wake of the suicide described earlier in this chapter, the student body came together in sympathy, and boundaries evaporated. People even talked about narrowing the cultural gap. A student-based organization dedicated to the cause was established. In spite of the student organization, the event repeated itself at the end of the decade.

When the researchers arrived early one morning in March 1989, the halls were in turmoil. Miami Haitian girls were wailing and sobbing in each other's arms. Advisors were guiding groups of students into their offices. The day before, the body of a Miami Haitian girl, Magalie, a senior, had been found floating in Biscayne Bay. Students and staff suspected suicide or foul play. She was a very pretty girl, tall and quite slim, who dressed exquisitely. She wanted to be a model and an agency in New York City had already expressed an interest in her. She had a boyfriend who was an upright guy. She was not an undercover in any way and readily spoke Creole in class, in front of African Americans. Although she was a newcomer, she was accepted by some of the African American girls because of her sophisticated style and good looks. Several months before, her mother had walked out of the house and never returned, leaving Magalie alone with her small sister. Reportedly, her stepfather was giving her problems. She asked her boyfriend to help her, but he declined to get involved with what seemed like a messy family situation. A Miami Haitian counselor who worked for a Dade County special task force concerned with the problems of Haitian refugees led a meeting for school faculty and staff where he spoke of the Haitian attitude toward grieving, how it is proper, even expected, to display grief in public, that it can actually be an insult to the dead to appear stoic and hide one's tears. The faculty and staff did not interfere with the Miami Haitians' public displays of grief. The tragedy pulled the student body, staff and teachers together in a manner not ordinarily seen at the school. Everyone, Miami Haitians, African Americans, whites Americans and Latinos, all expressed sympathy and concern. At least for the moment, one heard no comments on Haitians eating cat or African Americans being lazy. The tragedy jerked everyone together.

THE POWER AND CONTEXT
OF SEGMENTARY ASSIMILATION

During the 1980s, within the limited context of peer relations in this Miami inner-city high school, African Americans dominated the Miami Haitians. African American peer power encouraged many Miami Haitian adolescents to instantly assimilate, to commit cultural suicide by covering up their roots. While assimilation proceeded speedily, it was not into generic or mainstream American society. Rather it reflected the diversity of both American society and the assimilation experience. These Miami Haitian adolescents assimilate to a particular strain of American culture, that of inner-city, poor African-American youth. They have undergone segmentary assimilation, that is, assimilation to a particular segment of American society and culture.

Both context and power create segmentary, rather than mainstream, assimilation. The broader American societal context and the power it entails convince African Americans and, in turn, Miami Haitian adolescents that being black is the commanding feature of their identity. In America, regardless of what you say or believe, others will perceive and treat you first as a black person, a status that in the inner-city, poor experience of these adolescents is inferior to being white and superior to being Haitian. African American adolescents are educating their Miami Haitian peers as to their place in American society: if you're Haitian, you're at the bottom. If you are African American, you're just above the bottom, at least if you are poor and live in an inner city that is highly segregated and has had repeated racial disturbances throughout the 1980s.

The context for this segmentary assimilation is highly limited. Blacks do not dominate the business sector or the working sites that we studied, nor do they have much power anywhere in American society. Black immigrants, such as Haitians, who live in the suburbs and whose parents are middle-class are likely to assimilate to mainstream (that is, white American) culture as opposed to African American culture. Miami Haitians in the suburbs may still witness anti-Haitian prejudice, but their American peers and role models for assimilation are more likely to be white. Miami Haitians in the suburbs, especially if they are light-skinned, can escape much of the prejudice and discrimination directed at blacks in general and Haitians in particular. They are more able to interact as individuals with the broader American population, rather than as representatives of a disparaged, maligned black immigrant group. Those in the inner city, however, cannot escape being defined as black. They escape being Haitian, however, by assimilating to the immediate, local culture, that of poor, inner-city African American youth.

As Miami Haitians become successful cover-ups, as they begin to speak, walk, and look like African Americans, they gain acceptance from African Americans. The cover-up Miami Haitians have earned the right to be a part of the local society. This successful segmentary assimilation establishes the foundation for the Miami Haitians' next step, their reassertion of pride in their specifically Haitian heritage. Once Miami Haitians earn the respect of their African American peers, they can fling off their covers and reveal their true Haitian identity. They can wear Haitian clothes, eat Haitian food, speak Creole in front of African Americans, and declare to both African Americans and those Haitians who are still cover-ups, "I'm a real Haitian, girl!"

Segmentary assimilation gives individuals power to reassert their Haitian identity. The demographic majority Miami Haitians achieved by the 1990s provided a context that encouraged and protected assertions of Haitian identity. African Americans who had previously compelled assimilation now not only accepted those who had successfully assimilated, but also were compelled to accept expressions of the foreign, formerly disparaged culture. As in the workplace, immigrants struggled and negotiated with Americans over cultural forms of expression and control of their lives. The outcome depends on a shifting equilibrium of power affected by the larger society (for example, the perception that blacks are inferior) and more immediate contexts (the dominance of a particular group in a specific setting). The evolution of relations between Miami Haitian and African American in this inner-city high school demonstrates the continued importance of both race and class in America. Poor Miami Haitians confined to the inner-city interact with and assimilate to the culture of poor, inner-city African American youth. White immigrants, such as Miami Cubans, have different choices. Similarly, middle-class Miami Haitians, especially those who are light-skinned, also assimilate more to mainstream, white American culture.

The Miami Haitians who rediscover Haitian pride have prevailed over prejudice and pressures to assume a singular ethnic identity, either Haitian or African American. Instead, they have become self-conscious, multicultural individuals. They exhibit what has been called reactive formation ethnicity, the formation of ethnicity as a reaction to prejudice and discrimination (Portes and Stepick 1993). Yet, unlike other examples of reactive formation, Miami Haitians first assimilated; they first went through a stage of segmentary assimilation before they expressed their reactive formation ethnicity.

Those Miami Haitians most likely to attain the last stage, of reasserting Haitian pride, are those who are most successful within school, either academically or within American sports. Such success is certainly not achieved by all, either Miami Haitians or African Americans. Those Miami Haitians who do *not* make it in these terms are less likely to reaffirm pride in their Haitian ethnicity. They are the ones who may speak splendid black English yet have no interest in school. The ones who the teacher maintained are a problem no matter what. It is entirely possible that these Miami Haitians, the ones who have assimilated to the inner-city, poor, youth segment of African American culture but not to mainstream academic or athletic success, will conclude that they cannot escape prejudice and discrimination, that American racism will shatter their dreams of success in America. Some Miami Haitian youth will succeed and many have already. Others may not have the resources to evade the snares and obstacles confronting blacks in general and Miami Haitians in particular.

FIVE

Making It Work

Interaction, Power, and Accommodation in Inter-Ethnic Relations

"I'm a Miami native and I think this has gone far enough. Your comments are offensive and insulting. I hope the proper authorities read them and take appropriate action." The voice mail message was one of many critically responding to a *Miami Herald* newspaper article in which Alex Stepick asserted that in Miami American whites and blacks will either have to adapt, be tolerant, and become somewhat Latin American, feel uncomfortable, or leave (Viglucci 1997). In 1997, the Census Bureau reported that the population of Miami-Dade County grew at the sixth fastest rate of any county in the nation. At the same time, 142,000 more people left Miami for other parts of the United States than moved there from elsewhere in the country. By the year 2000, Miami-Dade County non-Hispanic whites had plunged by 22 percent from 1990 (Viglucci, Driscoll, and Henderson 2001). During the 1990s, African Americans also began to leave Miami-Dade County and were replaced by immigrant blacks. By the year 2000, Latinos constituted 57 percent of the county population, the highest percentage of any large county in the nation (Driscoll and Henderson 2001). In short, immigration propels Americans out of the area. Those leaving generally shared the sentiments expressed in the phone message. Miami was no longer the way they liked it, and they would rather leave than adapt.

For those opposed to immigration, Miami appears as their worst nightmare materialized, a harbinger of the future of the rest of America. Immigrants dominate demographically, politically, and economically. Spanish is ubiquitous, and many Americans believe that South Florida apparently has once again become part of the Latino cultural orbit, as it was when it was part of the Spanish colonial empire (Portes and Stepick 1993). To many, it seems as if Latino, specifically Cuban, culture has triumphed over American culture, that Denny's is an ethnic restaurant in Miami, and one must speak Spanish to get a job. These frustrated Americans refer to Miami as "Paradise Lost," as a *Time Magazine* cover proclaimed in the early 1980s.

Indeed, Miami does appear to be different, even upside down. First- and second-generation immigrants, rather than mainstream Americans, appear to control Miami's major institutions. Latin Americans, the newcomer immigrants, are on top. Because of the relatively privileged background of the first Cuban arrivals and the assistance afforded them by the U.S. government, Miami is the only U.S. city where Latino immigrants have created a successful and self-sustained ethnic economy in which they have a high likelihood of being able to work with co-ethnics in enterprises owned by co-ethnics, shop in stores owned and operated by co-ethnics, and obtain professional services from co-ethnics. By the early 1990s, just thirty years after Cubans began arriving, they controlled all of the most important elements of the local political machinery, and they had deeply penetrated the most important economic positions. Miami Cubans have the numbers, economic development, political power, cultural and linguistic presence, and social and psychological security to take center stage.

Most of Miami's blacks and native white leaders, along with some academics (U. S. Commission on Civil Rights 1982; Porter and Dunn

1984), commonly presume that Miami Cuban success has been at the expense of Miami's blacks. One black leader bluntly asserted, "It is a fact of life that Cubans displaced blacks." With a 1980 anti-bilingual, anti-multicultural referendum, Miami gave birth to the contemporary English Only, anti-immigrant movement that swept through other states with concentrations of immigrants. Each of the authors of this book has heard anti-Cuban, anti-immigrant ire privately expressed by members of Miami's white American business-civic elite.

Undoubtedly, immigrant influxes are associated with increased conflict. The Miami riot of 1989 was started when a white Colombian immigrant policeman shot and killed a black Caribbean immigrant motorcyclist in Miami's originally segregated neighborhood, Colored Town, now referred to as Overtown. In 2000, white American officials of the Immigration and Naturalization Service snatched the Cuban boy, Elián, from the Miami Little Havana home of his relatives to reunite him with his Cuban father. The raid provoked Latino street demonstrations and a strike, along with widespread anti-Cuban vehemence from both blacks and whites. Some Latinos apparently do not realize that there are other minorities in Miami, that African Americans not only preceded them, but also indirectly aided Miami's Cubans and other Latinos through the civil rights struggles that opened up the economy and society to minority participation. In 1996, after resigning from the Miami City Council, a Miami Cuban defeated an African American in a special election. No African Americans remained on the five-member city council. More symbolically, but equally hurtfully, in 1997 when Miami hosted a national Human Relations Conference on interethnic relations, the original steering committee had a majority of Latinos and no blacks. Public outrage led to the addition of African Americans. Poor relations between immigrants and established residents are certainly not limited to Miami, however. The 1992 Los Angeles riots incorporated African Americans, Latinos, and Koreans. In New York, racial and ethnic strife has included civil disorder in the Latino neighborhood of Washington Heights, conflict between African Americans and Hasidic Jews in

Crown Heights, black boycotts of Korean merchants, a series of inter-
racial killings, and a black protestor shooting and torching white and
Latino employees of a Jewish-owned clothing store in Harlem (Mollenkopf 1996).[1]

Violent, episodic events such as these encourage a resurgent nativism
and racism that include not only anti-affirmative action efforts, battles
against voting districts based on race, but also welfare reform that dis-
proportionately targets legal immigrants and native minorities. More
fundamentally, these battles embody questions concerning the nature of
America: Are we a single nation with a core of unifying beliefs? Or are
we subdivided into one-hundred-percent Americans and hyphenated
Americans? Are we moving toward unity or are our bonds balkanizing
into opposed interests? More specifically, will Miami become a fundamentally Latino city? Will it literally and essentially embody the Miami
Cuban joke that what they like so much about Miami is that it is so close
to the United States? Will the native-born, non-Hispanic white and
black Americans all leave Miami? Or will Miami echo earlier American
cities, such as New York and Chicago, that accepted and absorbed tens of
thousands of immigrants, yet remained thoroughly American? Will the
newcomers, the immigrants, still become American, but with an accent?

In the midst of the last great wave of immigration, in the early twentieth century, Parks and Burgess of the emerging Chicago school of immigration and urban studies assured America that conflict engendered
by massive immigration would eventually result in accommodation and
assimilation. Subsequently, the majority of academic and popular literature on immigrants has concentrated on assimilation, on whether individuals and groups of immigrants abandon their home culture and socially insular relationships in favor of American cultural habits and
social integration—such as how quickly immigrants learn English,
whether they identify with their home country as hyphenated Americans or simply as unqualified Americans. Previous analyses presumed
that if cultural differences diminished, if the immigrants became more
like Americans, then conflict would subside, and accommodation and

integration would follow. The focus has been on the immigrants, on how they respond, individually and as a group, to being in America.

Besides focusing on individual immigrants, those who lament the transformation of Miami have a normative perspective. Miami is not the way they want it, not the way it should be. The anti-immigrant and anti-multicultural literature from intellectuals such as Arthur Schlesinger Jr. (1992) and Roy Beck (1996) also reflects a normative perspective on what the authors feel should or fear might happen for the entire United States. Much of the literature from economists, such as George Borjas, similarly seeks to determine what is good and bad about immigration for the U.S. economy. Even the bulk of the academic literature on assimilation has an establishment bias, not distinguishing carefully enough what the authors believe *should* happen from what actually *does* happen to immigrants (Feagin and Feagin 1993).

As reflected in the title of Schlesinger's book, *The Disuniting of America*, Schlesinger and others presume that to be united, to be truly American, truly a nation, individuals in the United States can have only one true or fundamental identity at a time. ProjectUSA, an anti-immigration group, wants to "counter the growing presence of unassimilated, impenetrable, culturally antagonistic ethnic enclaves." Those who oppose multiculturalism in America fear that promoting or even permitting multiple cultural identities necessarily undermines American unity. They fear that if individuals identify as Polish Americans instead of just plain Americans, America will be less united. For the cultural conservatives, a few cultural separatists, such as Louis Farrakhan, provide easy targets, as they explicitly argue that America should be disunited, that different groups, such as African Americans, are so fundamentally distinct that American unity is impossible.

Our approach in this book is based upon different principles. Rather than beginning with a vision of what interethnic relations should be, we have sought to describe as accurately as possible what those relations really are. Rather than focusing on individual achievements and the actions of particular communities in Miami, we focus on interaction. We argue that the interaction between newcomer immigrants and Americans forges not only the identity of immigrants but also, and more importantly, the nature of America's self-identity. We are not the first to take this approach. Even the original assimilationists, such as Robert E. Park, at least mentioned the importance of relationships between immigrants and established resident Americans (Park and Burgess 1921). More recently, postmodernists have argued that "human identity does not have a fixed, permanent or essential quality. Identity is inherently emergent, always in process, and dependent on the assertion of difference through others" (Kibria 1998). More concretely, sociologists such as Omi and Winant have argued that "group identities necessarily form through interaction with other groups—through complicated experiences of conflict and cooperation—and in structural contexts of power" (Omi and Winant 1994, 511).

We apply these general arguments to the concrete case of interactions in Miami between newcomer immigrants and established residents. We argue that the existence of ethnic enclaves, Miami's Little Havana or Little Haiti, tells us less about what Miami is than the interaction between Miami's Cubans, Miami's Haitians, and the rest of Miami. We believe that the real impact of the cultural expressions of immigrants and native minorities depends upon how others respond. The existence of Little Havana and the Latin Chamber of Commerce is important, but even more important is how broader Miami and the dominant Greater Miami Chamber of Commerce respond. The dominant white American response, and in turn Miami Cubans' responses to them, will determine if Latinos and white Americans further separate or converge.

Miami Americans through the early 1980s maintained traditional U.S. assimilationist expectations. Miami's white American business and civic elite bemoaned Miami Cuban immigrants' persistent Spanish and their focus on Cuban rather than U.S. politics. But they expressed faith that Miami's Cubans would follow the pattern of earlier immigrants, that with time the use of Spanish and the focus on the homeland would decline, and they would assimilate to American culture.

By the late 1980s, however, they changed their expectations. Rather than expecting Miami Cubans to become Americanized, many engaged in reverse acculturation; they heralded Miami as the capital of Latin America, and they began to learn Spanish and to adopt Miami Cuban and Latino culture. Similarly, adult Haitian immigrants in the apparel factories and hotels are likely to learn some Spanish.

Miami's Americans did not abandon the goals of assimilation and become multiculturalists just because they enjoy cultural diversity. The transformation was occasioned by a shift in power relations. The local power of the Miami Cuban community reversed the normal flow of assimilation. The business and civic elite recognized that the economic advances of Miami Cubans and other Latinos made important economic links with Latin America. Rather than resisting the transformation, the business community sought to adapt. They engaged in reverse acculturation.

Reverse acculturation emphasizes the adaptation of the Americans. Yet the path of assimilation had not really changed direction from Anglo conformity to Latino conformity. Newcomer Cubans and other Latinos are also changing. The newcomer immigrants are still assimilating in important ways. While some white American CEOs are learning Spanish, English still predominates in the Chamber of Commerce meetings and in any event that brings together the top of the business and civic elite. Miami contains not just reverse acculturation, nor simply immigrant assimilation. Rather, Miami embodies transculturation, in which the newcomer immigrants and the Americans are changing, adapting to each other. Rather than degenerating into "impenetrable, culturally antagonistic ethnic enclaves," as ProjectUSA fears, Miami contains hybrid cultural mixes. In fact, Miami may be more of a melting pot than existed in other cities with earlier immigrants. White American CEOs stumble along in Spanish, while elected politicians mix Spanish and English depending on the audience. Miami Cuban restaurants are more prevalent than those serving American cuisine, but as in the rest of the United States, expensive restaurants are more likely to be French or Italian than anything else. In fact, this last point reveals that Miami may not be unique, but only illustrative and perhaps outstanding in the degree to which hybridity is manifest.

Some have argued that all cultures have always been hybrid, that there is no such thing as a pure culture. In fact, Rosaldo (1995) argues that most frequently people try to draw lines, create distinctions, between already shared cultures or aspects of culture. Certainly in the increasingly interconnected world, some aspects of culture are widely shared across borders. The Cuban business leaders now in Miami, for example, had ties with U.S. companies and U.S. culture while they were still in Cuba, before Castro's revolution exiled them to Miami. They may speak Spanish, prefer espresso Cuban coffee, and not quite begin their meetings at the same time as Americans, but most other aspects of their business culture they already shared with their Miami American counterparts. They knew about free enterprise, contracts, the importance of personal relationships, and all the other bits of knowledge that businesspeople need to know. Miami's Cubans and other Latinos were thus in some ways highly acculturated before they came to Miami. However, because they spoke a different language and came from different countries with presumably different cultures, Miami's white American business community presumed they were more different than they were. We do not want to deemphasize the importance of language and other cultural characteristics. These constituted, and continue to constitute, barriers. But as the ultimate incorporation of Latinos into the Greater Miami Chamber of Commerce and other business and civic institutions demonstrates, they are barriers that may hide cultural similarities, and that can be overcome when an effort is made.

While the dominant concern in Miami is with Latino–white American interaction, not everyone in Miami is learning Spanish and assimilating to Latino culture. Not all immigrants are alike, nor are all Americans alike. Miami Haitian adolescents attending inner-city schools in a poor neighborhood are more likely to adopt the dress and demeanor of inner-city African American youth than that of either Miami Cubans or mainstream white Americans. Haitians in Miami's inner city embody segmentary assimilation, in which they adopt the cultural styles not of mainstream, white America, but of a particular ethnic segment. Newly arrived Haitians from modest backgrounds do not encounter the America of prime-time television. Instead, they are thrust into the underside of America, an inner-city urban ghetto where everyone seems to be against them, from the highest reaches of the federal government to their peers in school. Through the 1980s, the majority hid their roots and assimilated to the segment of America that immediately surrounded them. They adopted the appearance and styles of inner-city, poor African American youth. They walked the walk and talked the talk, frequently so successfully that others did not know their Haitian roots. They successfully accomplished segmentary assimilation, assimilating to the African American segment of American society. In the process, they avoided the stigma and associated conflict that come with Haitian identity for youth in south Florida.

Segmentary assimilation reveals the importance of power within particular contexts. While white Americans may dominate national media, politics, business, and most other institutions, in particular local settings other groups can have power and influence. Miami's Haitian adolescents become African Americans because African Americans dominate them culturally in the high school they attend. African Americans are what Waters (1994) labels the immigrants' "proximal hosts." The phrase, however, does not sufficiently capture the importance of the power relationship. White Americans were the original proximal hosts of Miami's Cubans, but the rise to power of Miami Cubans changed the relationship. Effecting assimilation, whether segmentary, reverse, transcultural, or simply mainstream, requires power. Those assimilate do so, at least in part, because someone else has the power to set and enforce cultural and social standards. Usually white Americans have the power to effect assimilation. In Miami, at a broad level, Miami's Cubans reversed that relationship. However, in some social contexts, African Americans exercise limited power. African American youth styles have a great influence over youth styles for all Americans. In the inner cities, they utterly dominate and become the models for inner-city newcomer youth. Yet outside of the inner-city youth culture, African Americans obviously do not dominate. Haitian adults are more likely to learn Spanish than to speak in black English vernacular. Miami Cubans and Latino culture dominate the rest of Miami. Only for youth and only in the inner city do African Americans dominate and thus effect segmentary assimilation to African American culture among newcomer youth. In short, the dominant group to which newcomers must subordinate themselves and assimilate varies according to what group has power within a particular context.

We are not the first to emphasize the role of power in interethnic relations, but our perspective is different. Marxists and other power-conflict theorists have focused on power, but they did it in the same context in which assimilationists ignored power. Previous analyses of interethnic relations that center on power have always assumed or examined cases in which white Americans, Anglos, or in the case of Marxists, capitalists who happen to be of European descent, held and maintained power. Immigrants and minorities may have struggled for power, either through unionization or at the ballot box, but their victories were either absent or minimal (Cox 1948; Castells 1975; Castles 1986). Some political scientists and historians have highlighted the political gains immigrants made through ward politics, but even these were largely reversed by the American Anglo business-led reform movement of the 1920s (Stack 1979).

Our analysis of Miami differs in two ways. First, Miami reveals that immigrants can overcome relations of dominance. Miami Cubans' successes catapulted them over native African Americans into the white American boardrooms and backrooms of local power. Their arrival backstage caused great consternation and was certainly greeted with mixed emotions. Some white Americans resisted, and both Latinos and white Americans in organizations such as the Greater Miami Chamber of Commerce wrestled with whether the "Hispanics" should maintain their distinctiveness or thoroughly melt in.

Second, who has power can vary by context. White Americans generally exercise the power that effects assimilation. Miami, particularly in the business and political arenas, constitutes a particular context in which Miami Cubans exercise considerable power and have created a peculiar situation of cultural hybridity. Neither Miami Cubans nor any other Latino group exercises commensurate power in any other comparably sized urban area in the United States. Only in Miami have white Americans so thoroughly endorsed reverse acculturation. Within Miami's inner cities, African American youth exercise cultural power over Haitian immigrant youth. African American power is limited to inner-city youth culture and its relationship to Haitian immigrants. Overall, it is certainly much less powerful than either Miami Cuban and Latino culture in Miami or white American culture both in Miami and in the rest of the United States. Nevertheless, if you are a Haitian immigrant in the inner city, you are likely to acculturate in a way that reflects African American youth cultural norms of dress and speech.

While these examples are contextually bound, they reflect the diversity of assimilation and patterns of interaction. Rather than a single path of interaction and progress toward assimilation, newcomers assimilate and acculturate to whatever group dominates in a particular local context. Most areas of the United States do not have immigrants powerful enough to challenge the white American business leaders, but there are contexts in which immigrants or native minorities do have sufficient power to affect the process of interactions and the process of assimilation.

Miami also reveals that the old assimilationist emphasis on individual immigrants is insufficient and even misleading. Miami Cubans have certainly worked hard, and their individual accomplishments are impressive. However, those accomplishments resulted not only from their hard work but also from unprecedented federal benefits and the efforts of local white Americans to reach out to them and incorporate Cubans into local American business and political institutions. In contrast, individual Haitian immigrants have worked just as hard. Some Miami Haitians have achieved notable economic and political success. In 2000, Miami Haitians had gained political control of two small municipalities in Miami-Dade County and a single state legislature representative. Nevertheless, overall Miami's Haitians achieved much less than Miami's Cubans, who controlled the county commission, the largest municipalities, the county's delegation in the state legislature, and the countywide school board, along with influence in the county's most important business organizations. We argue that these differences reflect not just differences in individual characteristics. It is not that Miami Cubans have worked harder, are smarter, or get more education. What makes a difference both in the accomplishments of a particular group and in the nature of the overall community is the relative power of the local host community versus that of the particular groups of immigrants.

Perceptions and symbols of power and culture can actually be more important than the objective reality. The evidence of direct job competition between African Americans and immigrants is at best mixed. The General Accounting Office found that the 1986 law that required that employers check the immigration status of workers produced discrimination against Latinos, including immigrants, in favor of African Americans. Cubans in Miami did not directly displace blacks in the labor market. Rather, a new urban economy emerged in which the immigrants raced past the native black minority. A partial segmentation of the labor market occurred; a significant part, including apparel, was dominated by and seemingly reserved for Spanish-speakers, thus excluding native blacks and whites. African Americans and white Americans commonly assert that one needs to know Spanish to get a job. The most common refrain from those who support English Only is that no one in stores or service centers will speak English to them. Latinos, on the other hand, maintain that one needs to know English to get a good job, and research among first- and second-generation Latino high-school students in South Florida demonstrates that all of them over-whelmingly prefer to speak English over Spanish (Portes and Rumbaut 2001). To some degree, both the English Only supporters and the Latinos are right, and both are wrong. Objectively, many, although by no means all, entry-level jobs probably do give preference to Spanish-speakers. Yet a low glass ceiling restrains monolingual Spanish-speakers to low-paid, primarily low-skilled work.

While Cubans may not have directly displaced African Americans, and while English is still in high demand in the marketplace, Americans perceive that Cubans and the Spanish language threaten their jobs and culture. They respond defensively, some claiming that "there is no question that Cubans have displaced blacks" and others initiating the English Only movement. The perceptions of an ethnic base to the competition, however, are usually more apparent that real. As we saw in the apparel factory, conflict emerged when workers grabbed for themselves the easiest bundles to sew rather than taking them in order. The conflict is not inherently ethnic, not black versus white, immigrant versus American, or Latino versus black. Nevertheless, if the person slighted is ethnically different, the conflict assumes an ethnic cast, with blame likely being explained as evidence of fundamental ethnic differences. Throughout Miami, everyone seemingly assumes that ethnicity has something to do with everything, regardless of the objective reality. Thus, when conflict emerges, people attribute an ethnic base even when there is none. The "black-white" high-school girl was accused of abandoning her ethnic heritage rather than of attempting to become middle class. Latinos who speak Spanish in the elevator are resented for disrespecting American culture, rather than understanding that it is easier to use one's first language and that few people in elevators have conversations that include everyone. At the apparel factory, if conflicting workers are of different ethnicities, the problem is explained as ethnic instead of a problem in the organization of the workplace. Even if most of the conflicts over apparel bundles actually are between people of the same ethnicity, most

workers remember and interpret the majority of incidents as being ethnically based.

Socioeconomic class also fundamentally affects interactions. The
most common complaint Americans make against Miami Latinos concerns the pervasiveness of Spanish and the associated insensitivity of
Spanish speakers to monolingual English speakers. Those who fight the
hardest are working-class people, reflecting the importance of socioeconomic class in determining newcomer-American interactions. The
leaders of the English Only movement are not Miami's white American
elite, its elected officials or business leaders. Rather they are working-
class white Americans, some of whom are immigrants themselves. The
white American business-civic elite has never publicly supported English Only. Similarly, as early as the 1970s, working-class white Americans began abandoning Dade County for localities with fewer immigrants. During the 1980s, the same trend seems to have begun among
African Americans. While the black population grew during the 1980s,
all of the growth came from black immigrants. The elevated standing of
Cubans produced Miami's transculturation, and white Americans are
the most likely to engage in reverse acculturation. Working-class Americans, both white and black, are more likely to defend American culture
and resist reverse acculturation. Conversely, the economic isolation and
deprivation of the majority of Haitians thwarts the diffusion of Haitian
culture to others in Miami. Haitian Creole has economic advantages
only for social service personnel serving Haitians. The class position of
Haitians diminishes their power and their cultural influence.

While resentment and tension over newcomer-American interactions are common in Miami, on a day-to-day basis conflict is actually the
least common form of expression and interaction. Most usual are relatively conflict-free day-to-day relationships among all kinds of workers,
businesspeople, and students. Rather than conflict, the most common
response to competition is avoidance through ethnic self-segregation. If
given space and resources to maintain separation, most members of eth-

nic groups stick together. Coethnic workers hang out together and seldom interact with those who speak a different language or are perceived
to have different roots. At the apparel factory, for example, during lunch
virtually everyone sat in a well-established spot in the cafeteria, sharing
space with someone of his or her own ethnic group and conversing only
with others of his or her own group. Similarly, at the construction site,
workers ate lunch with members of their particular trade, who tended
to be of the same ethnicity. At the high school, Haitians ate mainly in
the cafeteria and African Americans off-campus. In the business community, until the mid- to late 1980s, the Greater Miami Chamber of
Commerce had few members other than non-Hispanic whites. Most
Cubans and other Latinos participated in COMACOL (for small businesses) or in the Latin Builders' Association (for large, influential
builders). African American businesspeople also had their separate business organization, the Miami-Dade Chamber of Commerce.

All of them explain their self-segregation as a response to discrimination from the locally dominant group. Haitian workers in the apparel
plant claim that Latinos do not allow them to sit with them at lunch.
Latino carpenters claim that the Anglos used to exclude them from their
informal lunch and after-hours get-togethers. Many Latino business
people feel that their interests can only be advanced in the Chamber of
Commerce by maintaining a separate Hispanic Affairs Committee.

Not just in Miami but nationwide, newcomer immigrants tend to be
segregated from the broader population. Demand for low-wage labor in
agriculture and other U.S. industries has channeled undocumented
workers into particular jobs. Many Mexican immigrants, for example,
confront stereotypes about what is suitable "Mexican work," generally
low-skilled, low-wage, unstable jobs (Portes and Rumbaut 1996). Social
networks tend to reinforce immigrant occupational concentration, as
most immigrants find jobs through friends already working in the same
place or at least the same industry.[2]

While a significant portion of the day-to-day, mundane reality of immigrants is segregated from the broader society, interaction does occur and mutual coexistence more than conflict marks day-to-day interaction. Interaction across normally segregated ethnic boundaries is usually institutionalized and thus is guided by regular, unwritten rules that allow superficial tolerance and the conduct of daily business. Chamber of Commerce members, for example, focus on issues that unite rather than divide them. They all want to improve the conditions for businesses in South Florida. They have all come to realize that the Latino presence has become a strategic advantage. Thus, the chamber does not support English Only, and it has sought to give Latino members positions of leadership and prominence. They also have unstated rules that discourage divisive ethnic issues. For example, rather than addressing the riots that occurred outside the meeting room of the New World Center Action Committee, the chairperson maintained that the issues were outside the committee's purview. The establishment of informal rules reflects the common-sense conclusion that most people would rather get on with their daily tasks than engage in conflict. Adherence to such rules produces seeming accord. These rules allow people to pursue their immediate tasks while regulating interaction across boundaries in safe, acceptable ways.

IMPROVING RELATIONS
Treating People Equally

People and institutions can also make a difference in lessening conflict. Most importantly, people must be treated as equals, a simple truth easily overlooked when confronted with cultural differences. The Greater Miami Chamber of Commerce became much more forceful and unified when it took the initiative to reach out to both Latinos and African Americans. Waiting for them to come to the chamber was not sufficient. Similarly, the carpenters union gained strength by incorporating Latinos. Even more importantly, when incorporating newcomers, they must be given positions of influence and power. They must not be treated as tokens. The unity of the chamber increased significantly when Latinos were elected as important committee chairs and eventually as president.

Treating people equally is not as simple as inviting them to the table. Especially those who have faced discrimination are likely to approach the table warily. Before they believe they are treated as equals, they must see demonstrable examples of respect for them and their background. The chamber's Hispanic Affairs Committee provided Latinos with a space that they controlled but which was sanctioned by the broader chamber. The celebration of Haitian culture in the high school permitted students to recognize that not everyone in the school was prejudiced against Haitians.

After participating in these ethnic-specific activities, people can come to the larger table with more confidence that they will be treated equally. Thus the multicultural wars that demand an either/or solution are misguided. Minorities should not learn only their own history. Nor should minorities be exposed only to mainstream culture. Rather both are required. Emphasis on minority contributions, a space for minorities provided by the majority, allows minorities to feel equal, to believe that they are not just tokens. Minority-specific activities are essential, but not sufficient to bring groups together and produce accord. They must be complemented with broader activities that bring all groups together.

Having a Stake

Not only must these broader activities incorporate everyone equally, but everyone must have a stake, must really care. Many multicultural activities, especially for adolescents, flounder because few of the students care about the activities. They are viewed as silly irrelevancies to their lives. Similarly, while the newcomer immigrant unionized carpenters deeply cared about the U. S. presidential elections, the white Americans were cynically alienated. On the other hand, in each arena we found some concerns that newcomers and Americans shared. Chamber of commerce members all expressed an intense interest in promoting business opportunities. Promoting a positive business climate prompted the Americans to overcome their impatience with Latinos' slow assimilation. Haitian and African American students expressed an equally profound interest in discussing their cultural roots.

Cooperative Activities

People can have a stake, be socially equal, and when in contact still argue and disagree. To produce harmonious relations, the activity that brings the people together should be one that requires cooperation, not competition. Miami businesspeople can much more successfully create a positive business environment, an affirmative image of Miami, if they cooperate. In the apparel factory, relationships among the workers were most harmonious when they joined together for celebrations of life and when they united to resist management. In the schools, after years of rejection, Haitians began playing American sports and demonstrated even more enthusiasm than many African American students on their school's sports teams. To win a high school game, everyone had to literally be on the same team.

In summary, newcomers and Americans successfully come together when: (1) each accorded the other equal status and fair treatment, rather than one waiting for the other to change; (2) both shared a sincere interest in some goal, rather than engaging in interaction because someone said they should, and (3) cooperation across groups was required to achieve the goal.

The Future

Immigrants are likely to continue coming to America, and America is likely to change. Conflict is also likely to continue, but conflict is not the primary mode of interaction between newcomers and Americans. Daily reality is much more mundane, with conflict being the aberration. Rather than seeing Miami as moving toward American or Latino cultural dominance, we argue that this struggle is producing a more oblique and subtle transformation, an Americanization of Latino culture, the production of a city that is profoundly, fundamentally American, but which has a Spanish accent and a Latino flavor. More specifically, American institutions—such as schools, workplaces, and political and business organizations—incorporate immigrants, adapt by addressing immigrants' concerns, and become bilingual or speak with an accent. However, the immigrants also adapt by accepting the terms of American institutions. Students learn and prefer to speak English. Workers show up to work on time and hope for but do not necessarily expect time off for family responsibilities. Business organizations usually begin their meetings on time and stick to their agendas. They have not fundamentally transformed America. They have occasioned episodic conflict, but they have also incorporated themselves into and even renewed American institutions.

Miami's Carneval (Miami uses the Spanish spelling of carnival) exemplifies this process. It appears to be Latino, a celebration imported from Latin countries and centered in Little Havana. It is the second-largest public festival in the United States after New Orleans' Mardi Gras. Every year around one million revelers pack the streets of Little Havana, dancing in the streets to the sounds of Latin bands spread across over thirty stages. Miami's Carneval, however, is not as Latin as it looks. First, the audience is certainly not all Cuban, nor even predominantly Latino. Carneval attracts everyone in South Florida—Cubans, Nicaraguans, other Latinos, African Americans, Anglos, Haitians. More importantly, the organizers are not the Cuban equivalent of the Hibernia Association (or some other recognizable ethnic association). The Little Havana Kiwanis Club organizes Carneval. Its members are primarily Cuban, but the organization is indisputably American, a prototypical American business association designed to perform civic duties while also promoting business interests. The festival itself is a long way from Brazil's raucous, raunchy version of Carneval. On the contrary, it is a very American festival with well-defined, even precise limits. Rather than taking place on Tuesday and disrupting the work week, it is on Saturday, a normal day off, with Sunday following for recovery. People can have a good time and they do not have to miss work. Miami's Carneval is domesticated.

At the same time, Miami also continues an unfortunate American trait of racial division. The most important, both positive and negative, role models for Haitians are African Americans. Haitians and African Americans are much closer to each other economically and politically than either is to any white group, whether newcomer or American. The nature of newcomer-American interaction is similar for all groups, but the content and the outcome are profoundly affected by race.

Our research leads us to conclude that Latino-American white transculturation and the associated accommodation will proceed, at least among the business and civic elite. We suspect that many working-class American whites will continue to resist transculturation, most likely by leaving the area. We also suspect that the force of American racism will result in second-generation black immigrants becoming primarily African American while maintaining limited expressions of their ethnic heritage, much like previous waves of European immigrants. We fear that conflict will continue along the racial divide, with blacks, both Americans and newcomers, being excluded from the emerging transcultural American-Latino Miami.

METHODOLOGY APPENDIX

This book began as the Miami component of a project sponsored by the Ford Foundation, Changing Relations Between Newcomers and Established Residents. That larger project took place in six cities: Philadelphia (Goode and Schneider 1994), Chicago (Conquergood 1992), Monterey Park in the greater Los Angeles area (Horton 1995), Houston (Hagan 1994), and Garden City, Kansas (Stull, Broadway, and Erickson 1992), along with Miami. It was designed specifically as an anthropological examination of the actual state of relations between newcomers and established residents. Part of the motivation for the project was the apparent paradox of widely reported conflict created by immigrants and grassroots organizations' claims that immigrants and Americans could and did frequently get along well. The board that designed the project felt that an accurate assessment could only be accomplished through direct observation of day-to-day, face-to-face interaction. The six cities of the broader Ford Foundation project were chosen because they provide different configurations of newcomer and established resident populations. Philadelphia and Chicago have significant concentrations of old, primarily European immigrants, that is, immigrants and their descendants who came in the great wave of immigration that ended in the 1920s. The other four cities were less affected by the old immigration, and new immigrants are predominant, that is, Latinos, Asians, and black Caribbean immigrants.

Each city selected arenas for study that would be most relevant for newcomer–established resident interaction. As described in chapter one, in Miami we selected the business community, work sites, and a high school. In at least one important aspect, Miami differs from many other U.S. cities. Miami is residentially and economically segregated to an extent that it is difficult to find neighborhoods where significant newcomer–established resident interactions occur. Philadelphia and Garden City also examined schools and the workplace. Other cities selected different arenas, such as electoral politics (Monterey Park), churches (Philadelphia and Houston), a neighborhood, and an apartment building (Chicago).

The fundamental methodology of the research was participant observation complemented by intensive interviewing. In each arena, our general approach was to first do some open-ended interviews, usually with gatekeepers to whom we had to explain our project in order to gain access. We exploited that opportunity to ask questions about relationships and generally obtained positive evaluations of these. If one were to rely solely on formal interviewing concerning relationships between newcomers and established residents in Miami, two contradictory images would emerge. On the one hand, those who represent important local institutions (such as the chamber of commerce or school principals) articulate a "can-do" approach, usually avoiding the language of conflict. Diversity, in this approach, is positive, and conflict can be managed. Others, particularly those who have little power and are in positions that are inherently competitive (such as apparel workers) often relate highly negative stereotypes of other groups, and blame these other groups (who could be either newcomers or established residents) as the source of Miami's problems, or at least the problems in a particular arena.

The subsequent participant observation provided numerous concrete examples that often contradicted the original interviews and provided guides for later intensive interviews, which were done toward the end of the research. At the work sites, the combination of participant observation among workers and interviews with managers revealed differences within the organization, as top-level managers glossed over established resident–newcomer differences while floor supervisors emphasized established resident–newcomer conflict. Participant observation revealed that established resident–newcomer and black-white conflict were undeniably present but largely controlled by the nature of the work and unwritten work culture.

In the business arena, the gatekeepers emphasized the extraordinary efforts and resultant success that the Greater Miami Chamber of Commerce (GMCC) had in integrating Latinos. While participant observation was limited among the highest levels of the business and civic elite, we did conduct participant observation at the slightly lower level of GMCC committees and functions, as well as in various organizations and groups connected with Castro's work as executive director of Greater Miami United (GMU). Participant observation revealed that the integration celebrated by the leaders of the GMCC was selective and was perceived by some of the Latinos as being more symbolic than real. When intensive interviews were later conducted with members of the civic and business elite, that knowledge drawn from the participant observation was incorporated into our questions, so that we could ask, for example, for people to comment on others' having said that "a Latin heading the GMCC is only a symbolic, token move."

In Edison High School, the sanguine view of administrators contrasted with the negative stereotypes of teachers and students. Our observations led us to the following interpretation of these apparently inconsistent perspectives: (1) high-level administrators believe it is important to present an image of harmony to outsiders; and (2) they have less day-to-day direct involvement in relationships among those below them, and may thus believe interactions are more harmonious that the reality we observed.

An inconsistency also arose between interview data from students, which revealed strongly held and widespread negative stereotypes of other groups, and observations of individuals from those very same groups interacting amicably and even intimately. We eventually posited a distinction between group and individual interactions: While group relationships were characterized by avoidance and tension, individuals from both groups could interact amicably and even intimately.

Another inconsistency between interview and observation data concerned the issue of becoming American. Interview data revealed little more than rhetorical recitations of freedom, liberty, and the land of opportunity. The only surprise in this data was that these concepts were equally common among newcomers and established resident blacks, as the latter group is frequently depicted as alienated and angry toward the larger society. But many aspects of American identity and culture are unselfconscious and revealed better through observation and reflection than direct interviewing. These include such things as rules for interaction between superiors and subordinates, expression of emotion, appropriate neighborliness, and treatment of public versus private areas. These could only be discovered by observation within a framework that conceived of culture as at least partially consisting of rules for behavior and interaction.

The participant observation also revealed how manifestations and mechanisms vary across arenas. For example, different groups can dominate or at least exercise significant influence within a particular arena. Established resident whites may remain in control of the most important sectors of Miami's economic, political, and cultural landscape, but other groups dominate in other areas. The extent of Latino influence in Miami is obvious and a pervading theme of the discourse of both newcomers and established residents. One area in which it appeared, somewhat surprisingly, was the apparel factory, which had established resident white top management and a predominantly newcomer Latino work force, who resisted management's imposition of established resident white work culture. Within the high school, established resident black students exercised cultural dominance over Haitian students, who felt compelled to adopt established resident black presentation of self-styles.

Data for the business arena was gathered in a number of settings. One important site for participant observation was the Greater Miami Chamber of Commerce (GMCC), the leading business organization in the area. GMCC did not give permission to project researchers to attend meetings until November 1988. After GMCC gave permission, two research assistants, Yetta Decklebaum and Christine Wines, both established resident whites, separately attended the meetings of different selected committees, including a black-oriented business revitalization committee, a committee that attempts to improve Miami's image, a committee which deals with international trade and has mostly Latino members, a committee concerned with downtown redevelopment that is reputed to be one of the most powerful groups in the area, and a small-business committee. At the time of the original research, one co-investigator, Max Castro, was executive director of an organization, Greater Miami United, that interacted primarily with Miami business leaders. He continued to attend the Hispanic Affairs Committee meetings, which he had been attending previously. He also attended annual GMCC conferences, where yearly goals are set and where much informal socializing takes place. One of the research assistants also attended the 1989 GMCC conference. Castro, a central figure in the English Plus referendum campaign and other efforts involving both Latino and non-Latino business leaders, conducted selected interviews with businessmen, read the local business press, and attended informal GMCC events. Through these activities, he came into daily contact with leaders throughout the city, including key business figures.

In the summer and fall of 1989, two co-investigators, Alex Stepick and Max Castro, began interviews of members of Miami's civic and business elite. For a sample, we began with a *Miami Herald* reputational study that identified the eighteen most powerful individuals in Dade County. We then crossed that with the membership of the Non-Group, a small, select, informal organization secretly created by the business elite in the early 1970s to discuss and confront Miami's greatest problems (the *Miami Herald* subsequently did some investigative reporting on the Non-Group, thus making it no longer a secret). This produced a list of thirteen people, all males, with eight established resident whites and five Latinos. We then selectively supplemented the list based on conversations with informed sources to reflect recent additions and deletions and to add some established resident blacks (no blacks appeared on the eighteen most powerful list). Our final list had twenty-one males, ten established resident whites, eight Latinos, and three established resident blacks. We interviewed all but four, three of whom were Latinos. We decided that, wherever possible, we would have the native Spanish-speaking co-investigator interview Latinos in hopes that they would be more comfortable with a native Spanish-speaker and thus more honest. Similarly, the established resident white American researcher interviewed those established resident whites who we felt would be least comfortable with a native Spanish-speaker. Whenever possible, the interviews were recorded, and extended notes were subsequently typed. For native English speakers, one of the graduate assistants attended the interview, did the recording, and typed up the notes.

With the permission of the Miami-Dade County public school system (then known simply as Dade County Public Schools), three researchers spent most of the 1988–89 school year at the school conducting observations and interviews. The observers included a Haitian-born male, Eddie Compas, an established resident white female, Peggy Nolan, supervised by a co-investigator, Marvin Dunn, who is an established resident African American. The team spent about three days a week at the school for most of the school year. Most of their time was spent in the classrooms, usually as assistants to the teachers. The observers also spent considerable time in hallways, at popular student gathering places on and off the school grounds, and in the teacher's lounge and work areas. These settings provided excellent opportunities for informal discussions with the staff and students. Classes observed included many hours of observations in English as a Second Language classes, where the most recently arrived Haitian students were placed until their English-speaking ability was sufficient to place them in the regular school program. We have also incorporated data from subsequent researchers in the Haitian community, Sue Chaffee, an established resident white, and Emmanuel Eugene, a newcomer Haitian. Stepick has conducted research in Miami's Haitian community since the early 1980s.

The research team in the school's arena was faced with a number of methodological issues, not the least of which was how to visually distinguish Haitian and American blacks. Haitian students who have been in the United States for a number of years or who were born here of Haitian immigrants do not stand out in any way. Nor was it possible to determine ethnic origin by merely listening to the students speak, since virtually all of the students who had been in the country for an extended period spoke with no discernible accent. This was obviously a concern in that often the observers were not in a position to know whom they were observing, especially in informal settings.

This issue was resolved by the team's decision to ask the students directly when in doubt about the ethnic origin of the student. Even this direct approach was somewhat questionable, since many Haitian students attempt to hide their ethnicity as a result of harassment from non-Haitian students. Still, the team was reasonably assured that most students were honest in answering the question.

Methodologically, the most crucial issue for the school research team was the integration of field observations with interviews, that is, determining the extent to which observed behavior coincided with answers given in the interviews. For example, if African American students generally reported that they did not like or did not spend time interacting with Haitian students, was this verified by field observations?

In order to assure that the same types of questions and issues were being addressed through field observations and interviews, the interview schedule was not developed and used until well into the school year, after the circumstances and conditions of interacting were better known to the team. Then interview questions were developed which were designed to probe the realities of the field setting. For example, it was noted often during the observations that Haitian and African American students appeared to spend more of their informal time interacting with students who were members of their own ethnic group. A series of questions designed to probe this field reality were included in the interview schedule.

The team was also concerned about the extent to which students would be influenced in their responses by the ethnicity of the interviewer. This was of particular concern in the instance of Haitian students, who were believed to be more defensive about their ethnic identity, feelings, and behavior. This problem was addressed by having Haitian students interviewed by a researcher who was Haitian-born. An established resident white interviewed African American students.

In the arena of work sites, the relationship that one of the co-investigators, Guillermo Grenier, director of the Center for Labor Research and Studies at Florida International University, had established with the union and management facilitated the initial contacts. The apparel plant was organized by the Amalgamated Clothing and Textile Union, and they arranged for Grenier and Stepick to meet the plant manager. Both the plant manager and the regional vice president were committed to exploring the production problems created by the ethnic differences at this plant. Grenier and Stepick conducted an interview with both of these men, during which they officially approved our project. Also at this time they informed us that this plant was one of the lowest producers in the corporation, and they suspected that this was primarily due to the ethnic and age composition of the workers in the plant. While they expected some production lag as their system was introduced, they had planned to undertake some sort of study, a survey they called it, to better understand the ethnic situation.

Grenier and Stepick interviewed all of management. In the process, we established a plant history dating back to the 1960s. The managerial interviews lasted from forty-five minutes to three hours. We also participated in various plant rituals, as well as regularly walking the floor, talking to operators, and visiting the lunchroom during the three different lunch periods. A middle-aged Haitian woman with some experience in the apparel industry worked both for us and in the factory from October 1988 through December 1989. During this time, one of the co-investigators would regularly debrief her in Haitian Creole. These debriefings were recorded, and subsequently English-language transcripts were made. Of particular interest was following her through the hiring process, since we previously had no data on how a Haitian would do in the procedure, which took into consideration mostly Hispanic workers.

Becoming a presence at the plant through our exhaustive interviews of management personnel also allowed us to become acquainted with other information that helped us flesh out the daily work experience of workers and managers. Of particular interest was the employment data provided to us by the personnel department and the production assistant. The former broke down the hiring periods in a way that allowed us to ascertain when each present employee was hired. The personnel department also made available the marital status and ethnic composition of the work force. We also had two research assistants who worked temporarily in the plant, Aline LaBorwit, an established resident white, and Bernadette Copée, a newcomer Haitian.

Fieldwork in Miami's construction industry was conducted on three fronts. Grenier had and continues to have a close relationship with the carpenters union, especially its Latino leadership. Two graduate assistants, a male and a female, obtained temporary jobs in the industry. The male, Steve Morris, who is a native speaker of Spanish, worked as a union carpenter's apprentice for one summer, while the established resident white female, Debbie Draznin, worked out of the construction union hall for two summers. She accompanied construction union business agents on their rounds of organized sites and organizers on their rounds of non-organized sites.

The carpenter's apprentice worked during the summer of 1988 and was officially designated as a dry-waller, although he never did any dry wall work. His work included laying insulation, installing seventy-five-foot vertical beams, applying studs, and a variety of other chores. The site, one of Miami's largest construction sites, was a half-million-square-foot addition to the Miami Beach Convention Center. During his time at the site, there were between one-hundred-twenty and slightly over three-hundred workers. Workers from diverse trades obviously participated, including electricians, plumbers, painters, masons, carpenters, and laborers. The diversity of trades at the site, as well as the number of workers of various ethnicities—established resident blacks and whites, newcomer Cubans and Haitians—made for a conglomeration rarely found at noncommercial work sites. Two graduate assistants, a Kenyan male student and an established resident white female conducted the research in the hotel and restaurant arena. The male, Hafidh Hafidh, had been working as a server in a hotel restaurant since May 1989, and the female, Debbie Draznin (who also worked in the construction arena), entered her site at an elite Miami Beach luxury hotel in October of 1989. She worked full time as a cashier in the hotel lobby gift shop. The server worked three eight-hour days a week.

NOTES

CHAPTER 1: BECOMING AMERICAN

1. The Ford Foundation's Changing Relations Project took place in Philadelphia, Chicago, Houston, Monterey Park (a suburb of Los Angeles), and Garden City, Kansas, along with Miami. Results from the broader project may be found in: Lamphere 1992, Lamphere, Stepick, and Grenier 1994, Goode and Schneider 1994; Hagan 1994; and Horton 1995.

2. Academic analysis of immigrant economic adaptation stresses immigrants' human capital, i.e., the education, skills, and work experience that individual immigrants bring with them or acquire in the United States. Human capital is the most important determinant of individual immigrant earnings (Alba and Nee 1997). Many immigrants arrive with human capital that may be higher than average for their compatriots in the home country, but is still lower than average in the United States. Not surprisingly, they tend to earn relatively little when they arrive, but with time their earnings match established residents with equivalent education, skills, and experience (Portes and Rumbaut 1996).

3. For greater detail on Miami's demographic changes and their political and economic impacts see Mohl 1983; Mohl 1985; Mohl 1986; Mohl 1989; Mohl 1990; Grenier and Stepick 1992; Portes and Stepick 1993; Lamphere, Stepick, and Grenier 1994; Logan, Alba, and McNulty 1994; Nijman 1996a; Nijman 1996b; Nijman 1997.

4. This compares to a national rate of 20.5 percent for both first- and second-generation immigrants, with 62.0 percent in Los Angeles and 54.3 percent in New York.

5. Significant numbers of Puerto Ricans also reside in Miami, but they are not immigrants.

6. The City of Miami is the largest municipality in Miami-Dade County.

7. Estimates of immigrant populations are notoriously unreliable. The U.S. census probably undercounts immigrants, especially those who may have an uncertain immigrant status. Conversely, immigrant organizations frequently overestimate their numbers.

8. Proposition 187, passed by California voters in November 1994, sought to prohibit state and local government agencies from providing publicly funded education, health care, welfare benefits, or social services to any undocumented immigrant. Implementation of nearly all provisions was permanently enjoined by the U. S. District Court in March 1998. Proposition 227, passed by California voters in June 1998, requires all public school instruction to be in English. It does provide for initial short-term English immersion programs "not normally exceeding one year." Although not applying specifically to immigrants, Proposition 209, passed in November 1996, was designed to eliminate affirmative action in California.

CHAPTER 2: COMPETING ELITES

1. In a separate program, in 1990 Miami-Dade Community College began a fellowship program that targeted black males. Students were given $10,000 for graduate school on the condition they follow up with a three-year teaching stint at Miami-Dade Community College.

2. These results are based upon a *Miami Herald* survey of 1,357 top positions in ten categories, including government, business, the arts, the media, law, and higher education (Branch-Brioso, Henderson, and Chardy 2000). The only area in which blacks were well represented was in top positions in higher education. But once the members of the executive board of the historically black Florida Memorial College are subtracted black presence virtually disappears in that area, too.

3. The state's affirmative action program for minority contracting—which sets voluntary targets for awarding contracts to women and minorities—

remains intact for some twenty state agencies and branches, ranging from the Departments of Agriculture, Education, and Insurance to the state court system and the Florida legislature. Governor Bush claimed his program dramatically increased spending with minority contractors, but critics claim that the governor's figures include contracts with noncertified minority firms and minority nonprofits (Whitefield 2000b).

CHAPTER 3: WORKING IN THE USA

1. As Lawson (1981) notes, "paternal employers attempt to join family and worker symbolically with themselves as the authority."

2. In Applebaum's 1981 analysis of construction worker autonomy, independence among workers was found to extend through the entire process of construction work, including control over one's own managerial supervision, the ability to regulate which partners to work with, and sovereignty to decide whether or not to work in adverse environmental conditions.

3. This joking is similar to that observed among longshoremen (Pilcher, 1972) where insults that in any other context would express and elicit hostility express and elicit friendliness and solidarity in the joking context.

CHAPTER 5: MAKING IT WORK

1. Immigrants and native minorities, of course, are not the same, nor are reactions to them. Scholars carefully distinguish nativism, which opposes internal minorities on the grounds of their foreign (i.e., un-American) connections, from racism, which refers to presumed physical and biological inferiorities among peoples. Thus, Americans could be anti-German during World Wars I and II, demanding the cessation of German-language schools prevalent in the Midwest, without being racist. Conversely, racism against African Americans marks American history without suggesting that African Americans maintain allegiance to a foreign nation.

2. Professional and entrepreneurial immigrants constitute important exceptions to immigrant occupational segregation. Over a third of all Indian and nearly a third of all Taiwanese immigrants are professionals (Portes and Rumbaut 1996). Many are engineers, medical doctors, and other highly skilled professionals whose jobs lead them to interact with the broader U. S. population.

REFERENCES

Alba, Richard , and Victor Nee. 1997. "Rethinking Assimilation Theory for a New Era of Immigration." *International Migration Review* 31, no. 4 (Winter): 826–74.

Andino, Alliniece T. 2001. "Speaker Remembers King as 'Radical and Influential.'" *Florida Times-Union*, January 13, B-1.

Applebaum, Herbert A. 1981. *Royal Blue: The Culture of Construction Workers.* New York: Holt, Rinehart and Winston.

Balmaseda, Liz. 2001a. "Grammys Bring Rare Harmony." *Miami Herald*, April 5.

———. 2001b. "A Whole New Tune on the Grammys." *Miami Herald*, February 15.

Barciela, Susana. 1993. "Minority Tenants Feel Abandoned by Bayside Mall." *Miami Herald*, August 10, 1A.

Barry, John. 1994. "Rising up Churches Are Leading Poor Areas Ignored by Banks to Power, Glory and Credit." *Miami Herald*, April 10, 1J.

Beck, Roy. 1996. *The Case Against Immigration.* New York: W. W. Norton & Company.

Bennett, Brad. 2000. "Civil Rights Coalition Not Resting Yet." *Miami Herald*, May 11, 3B.

Bosquet, Steve. 1999. "Governor Calls for Eliminating Set-Aside Plans." *Miami Herald*, November 10, 1A.

Boswell, Thomas D. 1994. "The Cubanization and Hispanicization of Metropolitan Miami." Vol. 46. Miami, Fl.: The Cuban American Policy Center.

Brackey, Harriet Johnson. 1998. "Denny's: Lockout Not Racially Driven." *Miami Herald*, March 5, 1C.

Bragg, Rick. 2000a. "Fight over Cuban Boy Leaves Scars in Miami." *New York Times*, June 30.

———. 2000b. "Legacy of a Cuban Boy: Miami City Hall Is Remade." *New York Times*, May 10.

Branch-Brioso, Karen. 2000a. "Fallout in S. Florida: Power Structure Shaken to the Core." *Miami Herald*, June 29.

———. 2000b. "Gauging Political Power Complicated in Poll." *Miami Herald*, September 4, 6A.

Branch-Brioso, Karen, Tim Henderson, and Alfonso Chardy. 2000. "The Real Power in Dade." *Miami Herald*, September 3, 1A.

Brimelow, Peter. 1995. *Alien Nation: Common Sense about America's Immigration Disaster.* New York: Random House.

Casimir, Leslie. 1998a. "Business Assistance Center Critics: Show Us the Money." *Miami Herald*, Neighbors NW 7.

———. 1998b. "Grant to Fund Overtown Business Revitalization." *Miami Herald*, Neighbors NC 3.

———. 1998c. "Warshaw Vows to Devise Plan to Help Overtown Residents." *Miami Herald*, November 12, Neighbors NC 3.

Castells, Manuel. 1975. "Immigrant Workers and Class Struggle in Advanced Capitalism: Western European Experience." *Politics and Society* 5, no. 1: 33–66.

Castles, Stephen. 1986. "The Guest-Worker in Western Europe: An Obituary." *International Migration Review* 20 (Winter): 761–68.

Castro, Max. 1992. "The Politics of Language." In *Miami Now!* edited by Guillermo Grenier and Alex Stepick, 109–32. Gainesville: University Press of Florida.

Castro, Max J., Margaret Haun, and Ana Roca. 1990. "The Official English Movement in Florida." In *Perspectives on Official English*, edited by Karen L. Adams and Daniel T. Brink, 151–60. Berlin: Mouton de Gruyte.

Chardy, Alfonso. 1998. "Reaching Out to Overtown." *Miami Herald*, March 9, 1B.

Charles, Jacqueline, and Curtis Morgan. 1997. "Success Doesn't Feel Equal." *Miami Herald*, November 30, 1A.

Colon, Yves. 1998. "Teele Backers Say Probe Is Racially Driven." *Miami Herald*, April 23, 1A.

Conquergood, Dwight. 1992. "Life in Big Red: Struggles and Accommodations in a Chicago Polyethnic Tenement." In *Structuring Diversity: Ethnographic Perspectives on the New Immigration*, edited by L. Lamphere. Chicago: University of Chicago Press.

Cordle, Ina Paiva. 1998. "Banking on Survival: Can a New Boss Turn People's National Around." *Miami Herald*, September 20, 1F.

———. 2000. "Peoples, Ventures Team Up." *Miami Herald*, May 4, 1C.

Cox, Oliver C. 1948. *Cast, Class and Race*. Garden City, N. Y.: Doubleday.

Crèvecoeur, Michel Guillaume Jean de. 1782. *Letters from an American Farmer*. Reprint 1925. New York: Albert and Charles Boni.

Cuban American National Foundation. 1987. "The Cuban-American Community and the *Miami Herald*." *Miami Herald*, October 19, 11A.

Davies, Frank. 2001. "Each Party Worried that Its Rival Might Gain from New Procedures." *Miami Herald*, March 11.

de Valle, Elaine. 2000. "CANF Adds to Its Leadership Ranks." *Miami Herald*, May 21.

DeFede, Jim. 2000. "Leave the Driving to CANF." *Miami New Times*, February 17.

Dinnerstein, Leonard, Roger L. Nichols, and Davd M. Reimers. 1979. *Natives and Strangers: Ethnic Groups and the Building of America*. New York: Oxford University Press.

Doris, Tony. 2000. "The Changing Face of Affirmative Action." *Daily Business Review*, January 12.

Doyle, Megan K. 2001. "Black Caucus Hears Top Democrats Call for Election Reforms." *Palm Beach Post*, February 28, 9A.

Driscoll, Amy. 2000. "Florida GOP Leaders Say Funds for UM in Doubt: Legislators Knock Choice of Shalala." *Miami Herald*, December 22, 1A.

Driscoll, Amy, and Tim Henderson. 2001. "In Dade, Latin Percentage Highest in Nation." *Miami Herald*, March 31.

Dunn, Marvin. 1997. *Black Miami in the Twentieth Century*. In *The Florida History and Culture Series*, edited by Raymond Arsenault and Gary Mormino. Gainesville: University Press of Florida, 1997.

DuPont, Dale K. 1998. "Stierheim's Legacy: Crisis Management Led to Real Tourism Progress." *Miami Herald*, July 19, 1F.

Espiritu, Yen Le. 1999. "Disciplines Unbound: Notes on Sociology and Ethnic Studies." *Contemporary Sociology* 28, no. 5: 510–14.

Farmer, Paul. 1994. *The Uses of Haiti.* Monrode, Maine: Common Courage Press.

Feagin, Joe R., and Clairece Booher Feagin. 1993. *Racial and Ethnic Relations.* 4th ed. Englewood Cliffs, N. J.: Prentice Hall.

Fernandez-Kelly, M. Patricia. 1994. "Divided Fates: Immigrant Children in a Restructured U. S. Economy." *International Migration Review* 28, no. 27: 662–89.

Fields, Gregg. 1995. "Success in America: A Minority View." *Miami Herald*, October 23, 24BM.

———. 1998. "Otis Pitts: Beefing up the Middle Class Is a Crucial Step to Revitalizing the Inner City." *Miami Herald*, June 22, Business Monday.

Filkins, Dexter. 1993. "Dade Basking in Glow of New 'Togetherness.' " *Miami Herald*, May 23, 1A.

Garcia, Beatrice. 1999. "Mission Accomplished—and More." *Miami Herald*, November 23, 1C.

Garreau, Joel. 1981. *The Nine Nations of North America.* New York: Houghton Mifflin.

George, Paul S. 1978. "Colored Town: Miami's Black Community, 1896–1930." *Florida Historical Quarterly* 56 (April): 432–47.

Glazer, Nathan. 1993. "School Wars: A Brief History of Multiculturalism in America." *Brookings Review* (Fall): 16–19.

Glazer, Nathan, and Daniel Patrick Moynihan. 1970. *Beyond the Melting Pot: The Negroes, Puerto Ricans, Jews, Italians, and Irish of New York City.* 2d ed. Cambridge, Mass.: MIT Press.

Goode, Judith, and Jo Anne Schneider. 1994. *Reshaping Ethnic and Racial Relations in Philadelphia : Immigrants in a Divided City.* Philadelphia: Temple University Press.

Gordon, Milton M. 1964. *Assimilation in American Life: The Role of Race, Religion, and National Origins.* New York: Oxford University Press.

Grant, Madison. 1916. *The Passing of the Great Race.* Reprint 1970, New York: Arnot Press and the New York Times.

Greene, Ronnie. 1998a. "A Bold Plan to Revive Urban Neighborhoods." *Miami Herald*, May 19, 1B.

———. 1998b. "Road Map for Change Task Force Suggests Ways to Help Poor." *Miami Herald,* May 13, 1B.

Greene, Victor R. 1968. *The Slavic Community on Strike: Immigrant Labor in Pennsylvania Anthracite.* Notre Dame, Ind.: Notre Dame University Press.

Grenier, Guillermo, and Alex Stepick. 1992. *Miami Now! Immigration, Ethnicity, and Social Change.* Gainesville: University Presses of Florida.

Hagan, Jacqueline Maria. 1994. *Deciding to Be Legal: A Maya Community in Houston.* Philadelphia: Temple University Press.

Higham, John. 1988. *Strangers in the Land: Patterns of American Nativism 1860– 1925.* 2d ed. New Brunswick, New Jersey: Rutgers University Press.

"Holding UM Hostage Hurts Us All." 2000. *Miami Herald,* December 27, 6B.

Horton, John. 1995. *The Politics of Diversity : Immigration, Resistance, and Change in Monterey Park, California.* Philadelphia: Temple University.

Hotchkin, Sheila. 2000. "NAACP Plans Lawsuit over Florida Voting Irregularities." *Associated Press State and Local Wire.*

"If Bush Loses Race, Brother Jeb May Be Held Responsible." 2000. *Florida Times-Union,* November 13, A-5.

Jones, Maldwyn Allen. 1960. *American Immigration.* Chicago: University of Chicago Press.

Kam, Dara. 2001. "Civil Rights Panel Questions Gov. Jeb Bush on Florida Election." *Associated Press State and Local Wire,* January 11.

Kasinitz, Philip. 1992. *Caribbean New York: Black Immigrants and the Politics of Race.* Ithaca, N. Y.: Cornell University Press.

Kauffman, Michelle. 2001. "Miami Wants to Give Event the Boot: Team from Cuba in Soccer Tourney." *Miami Herald,* April 13, 1A, 2A.

Kibria, Nazli. 1998. "Multiracial America and the New Immigration." *Society* 35, no. 6 (September/October): 84–88.

Kiger, Patrick J. 1997. "Squeeze Play: The United States, Cuba and the Helms-Burton Act." Washington, D. C.: The Center for Public Integrity.

Kivisto, Peter. 1990. "The Transplanted Then and Now: The Reorientation of Immigration Studies from the Chicago School to the New Social Theory." *Ethnic and Racial Studies* 13, no. 4: 455–81.

Kleinberg, Howard. 1998. "Overtown's Legacy of Neglect." *Miami Herald,* October 20, 17A.

Labissiere, Yves. 1995. "Coming to Terms with Black Men: Race and Ethnicity among Haitian American Youth in South Florida." Ph.D. dissertation, University of California at Santa Cruz.

Lamphere, Louise, ed. 1992. *Structuring Diversity: Ethnographic Perspectives on the New Immigration*. Chicago: University of Chicago Press.

Lamphere, Louise, Alex Stepick, and Guillermo Grenier, eds. 1994. *Newcomers in the Workplace: Immigrants and the Restructuring of the U. S. Economy*. Philadelphia: Temple University Press.

"A Latin Music Prize." 2001. *Miami Herald*, April 5.

Lawless, Robert. 1992. *Haiti's Bad Press*. New York: Schenkmann Press.

Lawrence, David. 1991. "Get on the Ball . . . Learn a Language." *Miami Herald*, March 24, 2C.

Lawson, Tony. 1981. "Paternalism and Labor Market Segmentation Theory." In *The Dynamics of Labor Market Segmentation*, edited by Frank Wilkinson. London: Academic Press.

Levin, Jordan. 2001. "The Latin Grammys Are Coming to Miami." *Miami Herald*, April 5.

Levine, Barry B. 1985. "The Capital of Latin America." *Wilson Quarterly* 47 (Winter): 46–73.

Lieberson, Stanley, and Arnold R. Silverman. 1965. "The Precipitants and Underlying Conditions of Race Riots." *American Sociological Review* 30 (December): 887–98.

"Little Evidence of Election Conspiracy." 2001. *Tampa Tribune*, January 13, 10.

Lizza, Ryan. 2000. "The Miami Herald's Cuban Problem: Between the Lines." *The New Republic Online*, May 15.

Logan, John, Richard Alba, and Thomas McNulty. 1994. "Ethnic Economies in Metropolitan Regions: Miami and Beyond." *Social Forces* 72 (March): 691–724.

Mailander, Jodi. 1996. "Why Did One School Cost Dade a Fortune." *Miami Herald*, June 27, 1B.

"Making Progress." 1999. *South Florida Business Journal*, April 16.

Marquis, Christopher. 2000. "Cuban American Lobby on the Defensive." *New York Times*, June 29.

McCormick, Clare. 1996. "An Incomplete Picture: Images of Haitians and Haitian Americans in the *Miami Herald*." Miami: Florida International University.

McQueen, Mike. 2000. "In the Cauldron." *American Journalism Review*, December 4.

McQueen, Mike, Tony Pugh, and Olympia Duhart. 1993. "Can Miami Halt Its Black Brain Drain?" *Miami Herald*, May 16, 1A.

Mintz, Sidney W. 1974. *Caribbean Transformations*. Baltimore, Md.: Johns Hopkins University Press.

"Misplaced Politics Shouldn't Affect UM's State Funding." 2000. *Miami Herald*, December 23, 6B.

Mittleberg, David, and Mary C. Waters. 1992. "The Process of Ethnogenesis among Haitian and Israeli Immigrants in the United States." *Ethnic and Racial Studies* 15, no. 3: 412–35.

Mohl, Raymond A. 1983. "Miami: The Ethnic Cauldron." In *Sunbelt Cities: Politics and Growth since World War II*, edited by Richard M. Bernard and Bradley R. Rice, 58–99. Austin: University of Texas Press.

———. 1985. "An Ethnic 'Boiling Pot': Cubans and Haitians in Miami." *The Journal of Ethnic Studies* 13, no. 2 (Summer): 51–74.

———. 1986. "The Politics of Ethnicity in Contemporary Miami." *Migration World* 14, no. 3.

———. 1987a. "Black Immigrants: Bahamians in Early Twentieth-Century Miami." *Florida Historical Quarterly* 65 (January): 271–97.

———. 1987b. "Trouble in Paradise: Race and Housing in Miami During the New Deal Era." *Prologue* 19: 7–21.

———. 1989. "Ethnic Politics in Miami, 1960–1986." In *Shades of the South: Essays on Ethnicity, Race, and the Urban South*, edited by Randall M. Miller and George E. Pozzetta. Boca Raton: Florida Atlantic Press.

———. 1990. "On the Edge: Blacks and Hispanics in Metropolitan Miami since 1959." *The Florida Historical Quarterly* (July).

Mollenkopf, John Hull. 1996. "Urban Political Conflicts and Alliances: The Case of New York." Paper presented at "Immigration Reform and the Browning of America: Tensions, Conflict, and Community Instability," Sanibel Island, Fl., January.

Molotch, Harvey. 1976. "The City as a Growth Machine." *American Journal of Sociology* 82: 309–30.

Moore, Deborah Dash. 1994. *To the Golden Cities : Pursuing the American Jewish Dream in Miami and L. A.* New York: Macmillan.

Morris, Steve. 1989. "Class Solidarity Versus Ethnic and Racial Divisiveness in Miami's Construction Industry." Santa Fe, N. M.: Conference on Applied Anthropology.

"The Myth of Perfect Democracy." 2000. *The Economist*, December 9, 8.

Nijman, Jan. 1996a. "Breaking the Rules: Miami in the Urban Hierarchy." *Urban Geography* 17, no. 1: 5–22.

———. 1996b. "Ethnicity, Class, and the Economic Internationalization of Miami." In *Social Polarization in Post-Industrial Metropolises*, edited by John O'Loughlin and J. Friedrichs, 283–300. Berlin and New York: Walter de Gruyter.

———. 1997. "Globalization to a Latin Beat: The Miami Growth Machine." *Annals of the American Academy of Political and Social Sciences* 551: 164–77.

"The Northwestern Debacle." 1996. *Miami Herald*, June 28, 20A.

Omi, Michael, and Howard Winant. 1994. *Racial Formation in the United States: From the 1960s to the 1990s.* 2d ed. New York and London: Routledge.

Parillo, Vincent N. 1994. "Diversity in America: A Sociohistorical Analysis." *Sociological Forum* 9, no. 4: 523–45.

Park, Robert Ezra, and Ernest Burgess. 1921. *Introduction to the Science of Sociology.* Chicago: University of Chicago Press.

Peacock, Walter Gillis, Betty Hearn Morrow, and Hugh Gladwin, eds. 1997. *Hurricane Andrew: Ethnicity, Gender and the Sociology of Disasters.* London and New York: Routledge.

Pilcher, William W. 1972. *The Portland Longshoremen: A Dispersed Urban Community.* New York: Holt, Rinehart and Winston.

Piore, Michael J. 1979. *Birds of Passage: Migrant Labor and Industrial Societies.* Cambridge: Cambridge University Press.

Porter, Bruce, and Marvin Dunn. 1984. *The Miami Riot of 1980: Crossing the Bounds.* Lexington, Mass.: D. C. Heath and Company.

Portes, Alejandro, and Dag MacLeod. 1996. "Educational Progress of Children of Immigrants: The Roles of Class, Ethnicity, and School Context." *Sociology of Education* 69 (October): 255—75.

Portes, Alejandro, and Rubén G. Rumbaut. 1996. *Immigrant America: A Portrait.* 2d ed. Berkeley: University of California Press.

———. 2001. *Legacies: The Story of the Immigrant Second Generation.* Berkeley and New York: University of California Press and Russell Sage Foundation.

Portes, Alejandro, and Alex Stepick. 1993. *City on the Edge: The Transformation of Miami.* Berkeley: University of California Press.

Portes, Alejandro, and Min Zhou. 1993. "The New Second Generation: Segmented Assimilation and Its Variants." *Annals of the American Academy of Political and Social Sciences* 530: 74–95.

———. 1994. "Should Immigrants Assimilate?" *The Public Interest* 63 (Summer): 18—33.

Pugh, Tony. 1994. "A Tough Sell Luring Blacks Back to Dade: One Year Later, Results Are Mixed." *Miami Herald*, May 8, 1A.

Rabin, Charles. 1999. "Beach Restaurateur Denies Discrimination." *Miami Herald*, November 12, 1B.

Reid, Paul. 2000. "Problems with Vote No Accident, Jackson Says." *The Palm Beach Post*, December 17, 25A.

Robinson, Andrea. 2000a. "Angry Activists Black Floridians: Our Efforts Were in Vain." *Miami Herald*, December 2, 15A.

———. 2000b. "Dade Trails State, Nation in Returning Census Queries." *Miami Herald*, April 5.

Robinson, Andrea, and Ana Acle. 2000. "*Herald* Ad Brings Afro-Centric Issues into Focus." *Miami Herald*, July 5, 8B.

Robles, Frances. 2000. "Elian Saga Awakens Activists to the Cause." *Miami Herald*, May 22.

Rosaldo, Renato. 1995. "Foreword." In *Hybrid Cultures: Strategies for Entering and Leaving Modernity*. Minneapolis: University of Minnesota Press.

Rudavsky, Shari. 2000. "Jewish Population Falls 7,000 in Broward." *Miami Herald*, August 12.

Schlesinger, Arthur M., Jr. 1992. *The Disuniting of America: Reflections on a Multicultural Society*. 2d ed. New York: W. W. Norton & Company.

Schroth and Associates. 2001. "Gore Won, Blacks Tell Poll." *Miami Herald*, February 20, 9.

Semple, Kirk. 1995. "Black in the Red." *Miami New Times*.

Stack, John F., Jr. 1979. *International Conflict in an American City: Boston's Irish, Italians, and Jews, 1935–1944*. Westport, Conn.: Greenwood Press.

Steinback, Robert. 1998. "Capitalism Is Black Solution." *Miami Herald*, September 8, 1B.

———. 2001. "Ethnic Groups Talk in Post-Elian Year." *Miami Herald*, March 11, 1B.

Stepick, Alex. 1996. "Pride, Prejudice and Poverty: Economic, Social, Political, and Cultural Capital among Haitians in Miami." In *Immigrants and Immigration Policy: Individual Skills, Family Ties, and Group Identities*, edited by Harriet Orcutt Duleep and Phanindra V. Wunnava. Greenwich, Conn.: JAI Press.

———. 1998. *Pride Against Prejudice: Haitians in the United States*. Boston: Allyn & Bacon.

Stepick, Alex, and Carol Dutton Stepick. 1994. "Preliminary Haitian Needs Assessment: Report to the City of Miami." Miami: Immigration and Ethnicity Institute, Florida International University.

Stull, Donald D., Michael J. Broadway, and Ken C. Erickson. 1992. "The Price of a Good Steak: Beef Packing and Its Consequences for Garden City, Kansas." In *Structuring Diversity: Ethnographic Perspectives on the New Immigration*, edited by Louise Lamphere. Chicago: University of Chicago Press.

Tanfani, Joseph. 1996. "Dade Gambles with Building Moratorium." *Miami Herald*, October 10, 1A.

Tatalovich, Raymond. 1995. *Nativism Reborn: The Official English Movement and the American States*. Lexington: The University Press of Kentucky.

U. S. Commission on Civil Rights. 1982. "Confronting Racial Isolation in Miami."

U. S. Immigration and Naturalization Service. 1997. *Statistical Yearbook of the Immigration and Naturalization Service, 1996*. Washington, D. C.: U. S. Government Printing Office.

Ungar, Sanford J. 1995. *Fresh Blood*. New York: Simon & Schuster.

Viglucci, Andres. 1997. "Immigrants Help Keep Dade Growing Despite Loss of Residents, Data Show." *Miami Herald*, March 24, 1A, 8A.

Viglucci, Andres, Geoff Doughert, and William Yardley. 2000. "Blacks' Votes Were Discarded at Higher Rates, Analysis Shows." *Miami Herald*, December 28, 1.

Viglucci, Andres, Amy Driscoll, and Tim Henderson. 2001. "How We've Changed: Hispanics Surpass Blacks as Florida's Largest Minority with Leaps in All 67 Counties." *Miami Herald*, March 28.

Viglucci, Andres, and Diana Marrero. 2000. "Poll Reveals Widening Split over Elian: Overwhelmingly, Non-Hispanics Differ from Cuban Americans in Miami-Dade." *Miami Herald*, April 9.

Viglucci, Andres, William Yardley, and Tim Henderson. 2001. "South Florida a Region in Flux: Young Families, Latin Immigrants Making Area Their Home." *Miami Herald*, May 23.

Waters, Mary. 1994. "Ethnic and Racial Identities of Second-Generation Black Immigrants in New York City." *International Migration Review* 28, no. 4 (Winter): 795–820.

———. 1999. *West Indian Immigrant Dreams and American Realities*. Cambridge, Mass.: Harvard University Press.

Weathersbee, Tonyaa. 2000. "Blacks Learned Hard Lessons About How the System Works." *Florida Times-Union*, December 18, B-7.

Weaver, Glenn. 1970. "Benjamin Franklin and the Pennsylvania Germans." In *The Aliens: A History of Ethnic Minorities in America*, edited by Leonard Dinnerstein and Frederick Cople Jaher. New York: Appleton-Century-Crofts, Meredith Corporation.

Whitefield, Mimi. 1998a. "Black Leaders Explore Path to Prosperity." *Miami Herald*, February 12, 1C.

———. 1998b. "Post-Riot Plan Went to Waste, Blacks Say." *Miami Herald*, September 10, 1C.

———. 2000a. "In Liberty City, Hope for Economic Rebirth: Investment, Less Crime Spur Area's Optimism." *Miami Herald*, May 14, 1A.

———. 2000b. "One Florida." *Miami Herald*, November 6, 6G.

———. 2000c. "One Florida Program Falls Short, Contractor Says." *Miami Herald*, November 6, 7G.

Wilcox, Thaddeus. 1994. "Shared Bank Branch Insults Black Community." *Miami Herald*, April 9, 30A, Readers' Forum.

Woldemikael, Telkemariam. 1989. *Becoming Black American: Haitians and American Institutions in Evanston, Illinois*. New York: AMS Press.

Wooldridge, Jane, and Gregg Fields. 1998. "Crisis Gives New, Old Leaders an Energy Jolt." *Miami Herald*, June 12, 1A.

Yanez, Luisa. 2001. "Brigade Ousts 2 for Trip to Cuba." *Miami Herald*, April 9.

Yardley, William, and Jason Grotto. 2001. "Loss of Whites a Stark Contrast to S. Florida's Growth." *Miami Herald*, March 29.

Yearwood, Lori. 1998. "Black People Have to Be Responsible for Their Community." *Miami Herald*, September 12, 1G.

Zangwill, Israel. 1921. *The Melting Pot: Drama in Four Acts*. New York: Macmillan.

INDEX

Abraham, David, 54
Affirmative action, 64–65
African American/Haitian student interactions: Haitian ethnicity perceived as a threat to black identity, 123; Haitians subject to prejudice, 114–115, 117–118, 122–123; some instances of positive interaction, 128–129. *See also* Haitian inner-city adolescents
African-American adolescents, 152; consciousness of racism among, 123–124; importance of black identity to, 124; as proud of American nationality, 123–124; as proximal hosts to Haitian immigrant students, 122, 146; school culture as the site of power of, 131. *See also* Inner city; Segmentary assimilation
African-American neighborhoods: federal government aid in, 63, 64, 66–67, 68–69, 70–71; Hurricane Andrew's effects on, 69–70; the inner city, 79–80; local economic development efforts in, 63–65, 82; rioting in, 61–62. *See also* Liberty City; Overtown

African Americans: black votes not counted in the 2000 election, 76, 77–78; boycott of tourism after Mandela snub, 65; business and professional class, 34, 64–67, 68, 70, 73–74, 87; class bias in responses to, 87; disaffection of following the 2000 election, 77–78; economic problems compared to success of Miami Cubans, 79–80; improvements in economic conditions of, 67–68; interaction with Caucasians (non-Hispanic), 81; occupying lower-level union jobs, 109; protesting dominance of Anglo and Cuban interests, 76; socioeconomic conditions of, 35, 62–63, 73–74, 149–150
AIDS, 116
Amalgamated Clothing and Textile Union, 165
American citizenship, vs. homeland identities, 126
Americanization. *See under* Assimilation
American national identity, multiculturalism and, 141–143
American values: newcomer appreciation for, 91, 154; new wave of immi-

Compositor: G & S Typesetters, Inc.
Text: 10/15 Janson
Display: Janson
Printer and Binder: Maple-Vail Manufacturing Group